Stories of Jesus

Contents

Jesus, Peter, John, and Judas

Jesus Teaches the Crowds

Love One Another

Important Lessons for Life

The Healing Power of Jesus

The Compassion of Jesus

Love of Nature

Truths from Nature

Introduction

Fr. Ron Lengwin

As a child I was fascinated by imagination even before I knew what it was. There are many examples, but one that stands out is the conclusion to John's Gospel when he states we don't have the full story of Jesus' life and that the world is not large enough to hold all the books that could be written about it. Imagine that!

Imagination is a wondrous creative power that can be expressed in many forms. When meditating or simply reflecting on a biblical passage or a complete story, it enables you to personally become a part of it and to learn and be inspired by that "participation."

Another form of imagination used in this book is to draw from your own experience of life, from how Divine Providence has unfolded in your life, from the Mystery of which we are all a part, from the presence of God within us. In that effort the stories of Jesus become our own. We understand them better, and that "revelation" opens a path to creativity that invites us to imagine what our heart and mind want to tell us without distorting truth.

In both approaches we are drawn closer to Jesus and all of those to whom he introduces us, especially his heavenly Father. Stories can inspire other stories, not canonically approved but still sources of blessing. Such stories begin within the heart of Jesus, whose presence within us speaks gently and openly to a soul prayerfully seeking his wisdom and love.

Faith and Imagination is the original title given to the group of stories in this book. They are a part of more than one thousand stories I have told on KDKA radio in Pittsburgh on a call-in talk show I have hosted for thirty-six years. The stories are used to introduce the guest and topic for the evening. The program is called "Amplify" and is identified as one that looks at life from a religious perspective. KDKA is the world's first commercial radio station.

These stories have been given to me by Connie Ann Valenti, with whom I have been the best of friends for nearly forty years. She is a woman of great faith and deep imagination and is the first person to tell you that they are not her stories but gifts given to her to be shared with us.

When I ask for a story, she blesses herself in order to place herself in the presence of God, calls upon the assistance of the heavens, and then recites a story, which I record. Any editing I might perform is minimal. In her generous spirit she gives me more credit than I deserve for these stories.

The radio provided an ideal approach to these stories. Read the same way—one or maybe two at a time—these stories give the reader a "jumping off" point from which to engage his or her imagination and be transported back to the dusty roads, simple homes, and questioning crowds of Jesus' time.

The creative process is exciting. I believe imagination is a gift from God that can give form to what we have experienced in the depths of our being where faith is formed. Imagination is guided by the grace of God's inspiration without controlling it. In this sense imagination is rooted in faith. Together, both influence the mind and the heart.

Albert Einstein believed imagination is more important than knowledge. Saint Thomas Aquinas spoke often about its power. Like all gifts we receive from God, however, it must be developed. We can improve this creative ability by exercising it. We hope this book assists you in this effort and helps you to recognize how blessed is your life with God in every moment.

The Love in the Father's Heart

A Frightened Young Man

The crowd had slowly dwindled, but a young man remained behind. He would repeatedly walk close to Jesus and then stop and fall behind, looking around as if he were searching for someone. Peter said to John, "That young man seems troubled. He wants to speak to the Master, but I think we frighten him away." And so, he dismissed the other followers of Jesus, leaving Jesus standing alone.

Peter went up to the young man and said, "Come, I know you wish to speak to the Master and to do so in private." The young man nodded and walked with Peter toward Jesus. But the young man stumbled and fell to the ground. When Peter, bent with age, tried to help him up, a look of fright came upon his face. Peter said quickly, "I do not wish to hurt you."

Jesus said, "Get up, young man, and come to me. Peter means you no harm." With that, Peter left the young man as he stumbled to his feet and slowly walked a few steps to Jesus. "What troubles you?" Jesus asked.

Tears began to form in the young man's eyes and he answered: "Master, I do not know how to say this. But I have not always been a good man. I have been cruel to others, even my own family and servants. A high fever came upon me, Master, and I lay dying. All at once there was darkness. I could not see, and I seemed to be traveling very, very fast. And then suddenly there was a light, a beautiful light that seemed to surround me. I have never felt so much at peace. I heard a voice, which said, 'Arise.' And so, I got up. I did not see who was speaking to me, but the love that came forth brought great joy to my heart.

"Master, I was at peace. The voice said, 'You must go back. You must go back. You must change your ways and help others. You will know what you must do.' And then pain came upon my body like cloud burst. I felt as though I was awakening from a dream. For two days I lay in bed, and then the pain and fever seemed to break.

"When I looked at my family, I was sorry for all the trouble I had caused them. My cruelty had run rampant. My tongue had lashed out at the servants unmercifully. I worked them until they were completely exhausted. I knew I was wrong, even though my wife told me, 'You must have pity and compassion on them for they are like us.' She had heard you speak many times. And now I know, Master, that I must have been in the Father's home."

Jesus placed his hand on the young man's shoulder and said, "My friend, my friend, did that have to happen to change you?"

"Yes," the young man answered.

Jesus said, "Then I implore you to remember what has been given to you and go and teach others and show them compassion by your actions."

Then Jesus looked down at the earth and drew three circles on it, saying, "One is the world, the second is humanity, and the third is the Father of us all. The three are circles of love within the Father's heart. He loves all of us. He did not create one person better or worse than another, and so no one should be a slave of another. Go in peace and teach others what you have learned."

Walking through Life to God

*J*esus sat and looked at the crowd of people gathering in front of him. Some of them had traveled many miles to see him—some simply out of curiosity and others in pursuit of hopes and dreams. There were many different kinds of people—some wise, some humble, some proud. The deaf, the dumb, and the blind were also among them.

Peter was getting nervous watching Jesus slowly scan the small group of men, women, and children because Jesus had not spoken a single word to them. But suddenly an old man cleared his throat rather nervously and said softly and humbly: "Master, I'm old, tired, and hungry. I have traveled a long distance to listen to you teach, and you have not said anything. Is this all I've come for?"

Jesus smiled gently and said, "My friend, is there something you would like to ask me?"

The man thought for awhile and then said, "Master, if there were only one gift that all of us could receive from you today, what should we ask for?"

Jesus answered: "Inner peace, an inner peace."

A younger man spoke out and said, "Why not riches, authority, power, happiness, or children?"

Jesus shook his head from side to side and answered: "Inner peace brings happiness, joy, and fulfillment. Most of all, it brings us closer to the Father. We suffer much pain in life, and much of it comes from our family. There is joy in family life, but there is also pain when a loved one leaves us."

And then Jesus bent down and picked up small pebbles until he had a handful. He got up and began to pass them out to selected people in the crowd. They stared at him and wondered what he was doing. Some were happy to receive this simple gift, and others were surprised, perplexed, or even troubled.

Jesus said: "The stones I have given you are light to carry. They are like some of life's troubles and burdens. But place one in your sandal, and it will cause you pain. Place it in your mouth and chew on it, and you will hurt yourself. The same thing happens when we place troubles in the heart or mind."

Then he looked down at his hands and said: "My hands are dirty from the earth. All of us dirty our hands at times. And all of us can find happiness, for it is a gift offered to each of us. Even though there may be pain or sorrow in life, when you walk with the Father, you will receive inner peace and joy. No matter what people may think or what their heart may tell them, there is no better person to walk through life with than the Father."

Turning to Friends in Trouble

Jesus seemed pleased even though the crowd was very small. He was tired because he had spoken for a long time and had walked many miles. His friends were pleased because they knew that even though the crowd was small, Jesus would be asked many questions.

Among the group was a young man who said, "Master, when a man has troubles, to whom should he turn? Should he seek out his father, or his brother, his neighbor? Or should he go to the temple?" Jesus was silent, and so the young man asked, "Can't you answer me?"

Jesus remained silent. The men looked at one another. Peter became a little nervous and said to John, "Why hasn't the Master answered him?"

John replied, "Patience, the Master will address him in time."

Jesus sighed and said, "My friend, to whom do you go?"

The man began to laugh and answered, "I go to my friend."

"And does your friend help you?" Jesus asked.

"Sometimes. When it is a business problem, I go to my neighbor or my father, but I go to someone I know I can trust," the man replied.

Jesus nodded his head and said, "I ask you, then, is there not someone that can give you an answer, someone that you can trust? The answer may not always be pleasing, and you may hear it only in your heart."

The man looked straight at Jesus and said: "I do not understand you. I came here in good faith. I'm asking you a question, but you speak in riddles."

Jesus looked down at the earth, scooped up a handful, let it slowly flow through his fingers, and said: "You are a man of great wealth. I know that you have learned much from many people, but you have not learned one valuable lesson. And that is how to ask the Father for help, for inspiration, and for guidance."

The man sighed and said: "I go to the temple. I am a good Jew."

Jesus replied, "You only speak, my friend, but you do not understand your own words. I tell you that the Father, the Creator of us all, will help you. It is not wrong, and in fact many times it is wise to ask another for help. But you should also ask the Father for help because he is wisdom and love and possesses gifts beyond gifts."

Then Jesus looked down at the earth and said, "Remember, when the time comes for judgment, will you have already felt the love of the Father and spoken to him, or will it be the first time?"

Forget the Pain

*J*esus felt sad as a woman cursed him through her tear-filled eyes. Her husband tried to quiet her, but to no avail. When she was finished, she fell down upon her knees in exhaustion. Her anger was gone but not the feeling of loss and pain.

Her husband asked Jesus: "Why? We have lived good lives. We have been faithful and yet our only child, a male child, has died. It was a difficult death, Master. He cried out in pain, but there was nothing we could do to comfort him. I had to work in the fields, and when I came home exhausted, my wife would not greet me at the door. No bread was baked. Only through the generosity of our neighbors did we eat, for my wife held our son, it seemed for many months, comforting him as he cried out in pain that tore at her heart each and every day until I could stand it no longer.

"Yes, I cursed the Father, and when I did, Master, my son looked at me and through his tears said weakly, 'Father, Father, be not angry, hold no anger in your heart.' I asked him why. Did he know what he was putting us through when he cried out and didn't he understand that we too felt his suffering? He told me that at times he saw a shadowy figure who would give him comfort and a deep sleep, but it did not last long. He was not afraid to die and would in fact welcome it. Soon after that, Master, he died in my wife's arms. But why did he have such pain and suffering? Is there no mercy? Does God not understand human pain?"

Jesus stretched out his arms and said: "My children, when we sin or are in pain, the Father understands. He feels what we feel; he knows all. Did he not create each and every one of us? I tell you this: There are many mysteries that we do not understand, many, many mysteries. But in time we shall receive that knowledge in his loving arms. He will tell us. The power to console you is not in my hands now. My words are like raindrops falling on barren, dry soil.

"Do not remember the pain," Jesus continued. "Think about your child in the good times, in the happier days, and remember the joy he gave you even though it was for a short time. I tell you this: When our time comes, we shall have no fear of death. My Father has told me that we should not fear death, for we will experience only peace and happiness when we join him and shed our earthly body of the heavy weight it carries."

☙

The Death of Parents

*J*esus saw a woman weeping at the well. He approached her quietly and said, "Woman, woman, why do you weep?"

"You do not understand," she answered. "I have lost my parents. I am alone. I have no one to love me and care for me."

Jesus extended his hand to the woman and said: "Many people love you, and many people need your love. Do you think you are the only one who has lost a parent?"

She turned around in anger and replied, "What right do you have to speak like that to me? You do not feel the sorrow I feel. Be silent and leave me alone."

But her words did not stop Jesus and he asked again, "Woman, are you the only one who has lost a parent?"

She responded again with anger, "What right does the Father have to take my parents from me?"

Jesus looked sternly at her and answered, "Woman, did you give life to your parents?"

She began to laugh at the absurdity of his question. Jesus continued, "It is the Father who has given us life, and one day we must return home to be judged, to be loved, and to be cared for."

The woman put down her jar of water rather roughly. All at once water began to seep from it. She cursed Jesus and said, "See what you have done?"

"No," Jesus replied, "see what you have done. Your heart is heavy, and so you want to blame and hurt others. There is nothing wrong with shedding tears, but you must ask when it is really necessary. Should you shed tears when the Father calls a loved one home? Do we shed those tears for others or for ourselves? We should be joyful.

"I know what it is to lose a parent. There were deep feelings of loss in my heart when my earthly father died, but I knew that he was being cared for and that he too would be judged wisely as any other man. Be comforted, woman. There is so much to life. One must take the bitter root with the sweetness of the honey."

Are We Born to Die?

esus approached a woman at the well. "I thirst, woman," he said to her. But she paid no attention to him. Again he said, "I thirst, woman." She still ignored him. Then Jesus sat down where she could see him and said a third time, "I thirst, woman." Without speaking, she poured him a cup of water and handed it to him.

Jesus thanked her and asked, "Can you not speak?"

She looked Jesus straight in the eye and answered, "I can speak, but I have many troubles. You do not understand, even though you claim to be the Father's son."

Jesus raised his hand and said: "Woman, woman, I did not make such a claim. That knowledge was given to me."

Tears slowly formed in the woman's eyes, and she said: "It was around this time of the year that I lost my mother, my father, and my son. This is not a joyful time for me but a time of great agony. I do not understand why we are born to die."

Jesus said, "Come, woman, and sit beside me." As she sat down, Jesus said, "Woman, do you not realize that there are many mysteries in life that we do not understand, that life is a precious gift from the Creator? While we are upon this earth, we are both teacher and student. We learn both good and evil from others. It is truly a gift to be able to make the right decision when there is so much confusion, pain, and suffering around us. Why were you born? You were born to give life."

"But it was taken from me," she quickly responded.

"Taken, yes," Jesus replied, "but that life did not belong to you alone. All life was created by the Father and belongs to the Father. Just as no person is a slave to another, no child is without the love of our heavenly Father."

She responded mockingly, "I guess I was born to give you a drink."

Jesus said: "Woman, woman, search your own mind. It is better to remain silent than to speak foolish words. Remember, all life is a precious gift. Each day we live is a precious moment. Each word that is spoken is a gift. Each word we hear can give us hope and help to fulfill our dreams. Words help us to grow in the likeness of the Father and give us knowledge to share with others. Remember to use your words wisely. Be careful in selecting your words and listening to the words of others. Work hard and give honor and love to the Father. To you I say, all men and women are gifts to be returned home to the Father with even greater love from their brothers and sisters."

Love Seeks Peace and Quiet

It had been a long and difficult day. The crowds did not seem to understand what Jesus was trying to teach them. He was tired, hungry, and worn—so much so that Peter was worried about him. He knew Jesus was weak from fasting and that he wanted to spend more time alone in prayer, but no matter where they went, people were crying out in need, and Jesus attended to them.

Jesus was walking a lot more slowly than usual, and so John said to Peter, "The Master looks very tired. We must take him away somewhere where he can rest."

And so, Simon and Judas called out to the crowd, "The Master is tired now. He will see you later."

In response, crying and wailing could be heard but also cursing and laughter. One person asked aloud: "How can he possibly be tired. After all, isn't he the son of a carpenter?"

Jesus ignored their complaints and slowly walked away with his disciples. They found peace and quiet in a friend's garden, but it was quickly broken by a loud, shrill cry and the foulest language Jesus had ever heard from a child. A nine year old stood in front of him and cursed him.

Jesus said firmly: "Be quiet. I am tired and do not want to hear what you are saying."

The child moved back three steps. Her father walked up to Jesus and said: "Master, Master, her heart has been blackened. She speaks like one possessed. Where have I gone wrong? Have I not listened to your Father's words and given to the poor?"

Jesus answered, "My friend, my friend, she has made her own choice. It was not a wise decision. After listening to those who speak about the power of evil, she thought she would become stronger by following their ways. She did grow stronger, but not in the ways of my Father. We are all free to make our own decisions, but those who have introduced her to evil will be judged for her pain and suffering."

When Jesus bent down toward her, the child snapped at him with her teeth, biting him on one hand hard enough to draw blood. Jesus said, "An animal that doesn't have love will tear the flesh of another without any reason. An animal, however, that has love may not back away, but it will not attack without cause."

At that moment a loud and hideous laugh came out of the girl, and she was freed from the bonds of darkness that held her. She began to cry. Jesus said to her, "Weep no more, my child. Nonetheless, you are as guilty as that demon standing near you because you did not use your mind or the strength that was given to you, and you did not pray for guidance." Then looking at the teeth marks and blood on his hand, he said, ""All men have done this to me and will continue to do so until the end of time. They may leave their marks on me, but I will place my mark upon my followers so that they can sit at my side forever."

It is said that when Jesus was returning to the heavens, the evil one met him on the way and asked rhetorically and mockingly: "What good was your faith, O Son of God? You have been beaten like an animal and crucified like a criminal. Your blood and your mother's tears have fallen upon the earth and dried. Your mother's heart has been broken. Your disciples are hiding in fear. And many of those whom you have taught, healed, and forgiven were among those who screamed for your death. What mountains has your faith moved, O Son of God?"

Jesus neither stopped nor looked his way but said loud enough for the evil one to hear, "My brother—and I call you brother because you were created by my Father—when you are sent to eternal darkness, the kingdom you have prepared for yourself and those who choose to follow you, you will have no mother to cry for you, no angels to sing of your glory, no people to cherish your memory in their hearts.

"Even now the name of your kingdom is used as a curse. Bask now in your darkness. The light will reveal you for who you really are. Faith's victories are not always immediate, but they are everlasting. You move the mountains. My Father prefers that I move people's hearts. That is the true miracle of faith."

The Love in Jesus' Heart

Jesus' Love for Joseph

Jesus was a grown man now, but he wept without shame at the bed of the man he called father. Joseph stirred ever so slightly, and Mary wondered if he knew they were with him. Tears fell from Jesus' red and swollen face. He touched his father's feet, and then he got up, moved alongside the bed, knelt down, and kissed his father's face. "My father, my father," he sobbed through his tears, "I love you so much. You have been kind and gentle to me—truly an inspiration. Your hands are rough and worn from hard work, but I never heard you complain."

And then, talking half to Mary and half to Joseph, he continued, holding his father's hand: "So rough from hard work but so gentle to those in need of your help—the man who needed something to support him when his leg could no longer hold the weight of his body, and the woman who needed a staff to guide her when her eyes could no longer show her the way. I resented having to pick up the wood shavings and carry them all to those who needed them to start a fire. I remember asking: 'If they need them so much, why don't they come to you? Why must we always go to them?' I also remember you teaching me: 'It is very difficult for some people to ask. It is easier for them, if you just give them what they need.'"

Jesus was crying so hard now that he had to blow his nose. Mary placed her arms around her son's shoulders and said, through her own tears, "My son, my son, I don't know if he hears us."

"I cannot tell either, Mother, " Jesus said, "but our memories and tears can cleanse our hearts."

Mary nodded in agreement and said, "I remember how angry I got with you when you didn't want to deliver the bread I had baked to a hungry family."

"You said I was selfish, Mother."

Mary smiled and said, "We have learned much together, my son, we have learned much together."

Then Mary's eyes turned toward Joseph, an old man now, a man who had been a father to her son and a husband to her, a man who made them a family. She thought back to the journey interrupted by her son's birth and how caring and concerned Joseph had been.

Her heart was filled now with a strange mixture of joy and sorrow as Jesus bent down once again and kissed the face and hands of Joseph and said: "Sleep, Father, sleep. I know in my heart there will be a special place for you in my Father's home when I return."

Jesus looked at Mary and said: "Mother, it will soon begin. You must be strong."

Mary said, "How can I?"

"Mother," Jesus said, "there is caring in your heart, and where there is caring, there is love. And if there is love, there is hope. You have taught me well, Mother, and now I must soon go to do my Father's work."

"You do not speak of Joseph's work, do you, my son?"

"In many ways, yes," Jesus said, "but in many ways, no. I have much to teach and much love to give in another manner."

<hr style="width:10%" />

Jesus Buries a Leper's Child

*J*esus looked at the woman whose face was swollen and tear stained. She cried out to him: "Master, I am unclean. Two days ago I gave birth to a child who died soon afterward, and I don't have enough strength to bury it." When Jesus came closer, she called louder: "Unclean, unclean."

Jesus said: "Woman, woman, only in the eyes of some are you unclean. In my Father's eyes you are special."

The leprous woman sighed and asked: "Master, is my child unclean? Did it die because I have sinned? Maybe it's a blessing because I could not care for it. I go hungry because I can't even care for myself."

Jesus looked at the covered form in the woman's arms. He bent down and uncovered it. It was not a pleasant sight, for the child was still covered with the blood from its birth. Then he covered the child's face again, looked at the woman, and said: "I shall bury it for you near a tree, a young tree that will bear fruit one day."

She nodded in agreement, and Jesus continued: "You gave this child life, but now it must return to the Father." Then he knelt down and scraped at the earth, first with a stick and then with a rock, until he had made a hole deep enough to hold the child. He gently placed the small body in the grave. Peter stood nearby but didn't say anything or offer to help.

Jesus covered the child with dirt, patted it down, and covered the grave with some stones that lay nearby. Jesus said to the woman: "When you see this tree grow, you will think of your child. My Father has been kind in allowing you to feel life in your womb."

"But it has also given me sadness," she said.

"Sadness, yes," Jesus said, "but without you this child could not have felt the warmth of the womb."

Jesus stretched out his arms to her, but she quickly backed away and cried: "Unclean, Master, unclean."

Jesus said: "Woman, woman, do you not understand? I am no longer afraid of you or your kind. I was at one time, but now I know my Father says we should not be frightened—cautious, yes, but frightened, no."

Peter said: "Master, you touched her child, and that is unclean."

Jesus shook his head and said: "Peter, is there no compassion in your heart? I will touch many with a worse disease—those covered with sin—even though not even one sore will be seen on their body. I would more gladly care for one covered with sores than touch a man filled with sin, but we should not turn away from either of them, for we are all precious in my Father's eye and he does not turn away from us."

A Lesson from a Rose

A young child came running up to Jesus. She extended her arms filled with roses for him. Her face beamed as Jesus thanked her, but she cast her eyes to the ground.

The little girl's mother walked slowly toward Jesus and said: "She cannot hear you nor can she speak to you, but she is a good child who is filled with so much love. When children taunt her, she may shed a tear, but she still shows them kindness in the midst of her sorrow. She never seems to hold a grudge against anyone. It is I, Master, who have a heavy heart. Anger wells up within me."

Jesus took the flowers from the little girl, bent down, kissed her forehead and thanked her, and then she and her mother turned and walked slowly away.

Judas said, "Master, the flowers she gave you are filled with thorns. Look at your hands."

Jesus looked at the little girl and said: "She carries thorns day in and day out. I will experience pain only as long as I hold the thorny rose."

Judas said, "Master, how can you be so forgiving?"

Jesus said in reply, "What would you have done?"

Judas answered: "When I saw the thorns, I would have thanked the girl and told her to keep the flowers. She picked them, and they were hers to keep."

Jesus said: "I saw the thorns, but she gave the flowers to me with love. To be given a rose is a beautiful gift, even though it has thorns, which can prick the skin and draw drops of blood. Life is like a thorny rose. Many times we cause others pain through our words and actions, even those we love who continue to love us despite the pain we have caused them."

Then Jesus looked down at a few petals that had fallen from his hand and said, "Judas, life has many mysteries. I think the rose was created for all of us."

Judas shook his head and said, "Master, I do not understand you."

Jesus replied, "It is to show us that there can be beauty even in pain."

Then Jesus broke the thorns from the stem of the rose, placed it to his lips, handed it to Judas, and said: "I give this gift to you Judas. What will you give to me?"

Judas picked up the stem, which still had thorns on it, and said, "Master, I have only this to give."

Jesus said, "Thy will be done."

☙

A Lost Job

A man sat quietly until all the others had left and then he went up to Jesus and said: "You preach love and caring, but my heart is filled with anger and sadness. I was a good worker. I was dependable and honest, but I was told to leave. No reason was given. I do not understand. Many of those who were not faithful to the master are still working. I have a family to feed and clothe. Why is there so much injustice? Master, look at me. Look deep into my eyes and you will see I was a faithful worker and servant." Tears began to form in his eyes, and then he began to curse.

Jesus stretched out his arms to the man, grabbed him by the shoulders, and said: "Do not curse. Why do you use the name of the Father in vain?"

The man looked straight into Jesus' eyes and replied, "How can I be faithful and have love in my heart when I am not sure where the next meal will come from or if I will be able to provide shelter for my family? Did you not hear me when I said that I was a faithful servant? I worked hard and gave my all. And yet with a few words I was dismissed. There was no caring. It was as if I didn't even exist."

Jesus said: "Life has many mysteries. You do not know what was in the heart and mind of your master, whom you have served well."

"Greed," the man quickly replied. "He was able to find someone to do the work cheaper than I would. He is tight with the coin."

"This may be so," Jesus replied, "but to curse him is wrong. You must find another master and do good work for him."

The man shook his head and said, "I will never give my all again, for many years are upon me. I am no longer young, even though I still have much responsibility."

Jesus said: "Then faith must be your crutch. Faith and prayer, and then you must seek ways to work for others."

Jesus looked at him a moment more and then began to turn to leave. He paused and said: "The world is large, my friend. There is much work to be done in many places for a man who is skilled and caring—a man who will respect his master and do good work. You have been hurt by your dismissal, but you can change your life. My friend, my friend, have faith and you will find another master who will respect you as you respect him."

Love Expects Little in Return

*J*esus sat down after what had been a long and tiring but still pleasant day. He watched intently as the sun slowly slid out of sight into the heavens. Peter said to him, "Master, who was the woman you spoke to today?"

Jesus answered, "I spoke to many women."

Peter replied, "Master, I think you know the one I mean because I saw great love and caring in your eyes for her."

Jesus smiled and said: "Yes, I know the woman of whom you speak. She has spent her entire life comforting the sick. She has given so much of herself and has received so little in return. Her love for others is strong. When she helped my mother care for my father long ago, she said, 'I give because it pleases me. I know that in addition to the great joy I receive on earth, I shall receive even more when I die.' I asked her if that was the only reason she healed others. She looked at me, smiled, and answered: 'My friend, I do it because they are my brothers and sisters. If we do not care for one another, who will care for us? You are a young man, and you learn from others, do you not?' Yes, Peter, she taught me a great lesson. She was a woman who gave so much to others and expected very little in return from them."

Peter shook his head and said, "She is very much like you, Master."

Jesus smiled again and responded, "I had a great teacher, Peter, and I hope you will remember and pass on to others what I have taught you."

A Basket Filled with Love

*F*or the second day in a row a group of men gathered to listen to Jesus and ask him questions. Peter was concerned that there would not be any food to give them and said, "I pray the women will bring us bread and some fruit."

Jesus replied, "Have no fear, Peter."

Peter responded: "But this is the second day that we have had to feed this group. Will the women continue to bring us bread as they have before?"

"Have no fear, Peter," Jesus said once again.

When Peter turned and grumbled, John said, "Peter, Peter, have you no faith?" And he began to laugh. Peter showed that he was angry in the way he walked and by the look on his face. He caught up with John and said, "John, this is the second day that this group has been with us, and if the women do not bring bread and fruit, we may have an angry crowd to contend with."

John looked serious now when he turned toward Peter and asked again, "Have you no faith, Peter?"

Peter looked at him and answered, "Faith I have, but with the women I am not sure." Even as he was speaking, three women came carrying baskets with bread and fruit in them.

After everyone had eaten, Jesus began to speak about love and caring and the strength they provide. "When one loves," he said, "one's bond with the Father is strong. We should love our neighbors as we love ourselves, because each of us is like a golden light in my Father's home. We are connected to him as a child is connected to its mother's womb."

Jesus continued speaking about love, and when he was finished, the crowd slowly began to disperse. But one old man turned around and asked, "Master, may I speak with you privately?"

"Yes," Jesus answered. "Come." And they both sat down near an olive tree.

The old man said to Jesus: "This was not the first nor do I hope it will be the last time I listen to you. You speak often about loving, caring, and sharing. Why is it so important to live this way?"

Jesus smiled and answered: "When we enter the gates of the heavens after our life on earth has ended, we carry with us a basket that can only be seen by us and the angels. In it is the love that we shared with others—what we have given to others, how we listened to others, how we helped others and taught others, showing them how to grow.

"When we present this basket, it is carried by the angels to the heavenly Father. Do you want to present a basket that is empty, revealing that you have never shared love, never cared for others, never listened to others' problems and concerns, never comforted others with your words, never extended your hands to help others?"

The old man looked down at the ground and then up at Jesus and answered: "Master, your words are so simple, but should I really believe you? What you say makes sense, but why should I believe everything that you tell me?"

Jesus smiled again and answered, "My friend, my friend, you have free will to believe or not to believe me, but that child is foolish who does not care if his basket will be empty or will be filled with love and caring."

The old man smiled and said, "You have made your point, my friend, you have made your point."

Where Is the Justice?

A group of men gathered. It was a beautiful day. There was not a cloud in the sky. One of the men stood in the back, behind everyone else. After Jesus had finished speaking and the crowd was leaving, he came forward and said to Jesus, "Master, I have a question to ask you."

Peter complained, "Well, why didn't you ask it before?"

The man looked at Peter with anger and replied, "This is between the Master and me."

Jesus knew the man was angry. He shook his head and said, "We are all brothers here. What you say to me, you can say in front of my friends."

The man responded abruptly, "Then sit down and listen to me." And so, Jesus, Peter and John sat down.

The man continued, "There is much anger and hate in me." Jesus nodded his head in agreement. "My brother and I were fishermen, but my brother is no longer with us. One day I was ill and could not go fishing with him. So, he and two of my sons went and cast their nets in the sea. As they were doing this, a storm suddenly arose, the boat capsized, and they all drowned. Why did they drown? They were much better than I am. They worshiped in the temple, gave alms to the poor, and shared their fish with widows and their families to feed their hungry bellies. Why was I spared and they were not?"

Jesus thought for a moment, sighed, and then answered: "The storm did not arise from the anger of my heavenly Father. It was from nature. It was their time to go."

"Oh," the man responded, "so nature and God work hand in hand?"

Jesus answered, "No." Then he said again, "It was their time."

"Yes," the man responded cynically and with great emotion, "the storm came up and the waters swallowed them. You are called 'the wise man.' Where is the justice in that?"

Jesus answered, "There is much hurt and anger in you. No matter what I say to you now, you will not understand the true meaning of my words. I could tell by the way you approached me that you were full of anger. I tell you this, my son. The anger within you is like the power of the storm that caused the boat to capsize. When you learn to calm yourself, you will understand my words."

Then Jesus got up slowly and walked away. Peter and John hurried to catch up to him. John said, "Master, you gave no comfort to that man."

Jesus replied, "I answered to the best of my ability."

Peter noticed the tears that were slowly forming in Jesus' eyes and asked, "Master, why do you weep?"

Jesus answered, "I weep for all humankind. The kind of anger that this man holds in his heart, mind, and body can cause more destruction than the sea, the earth or the winds."

Love Flows from Jesus

A young man came to spend some time with Jesus because his mother and father had told him about some of the wonders Jesus had performed—a man who could heal the sick and raise the dead, who could make people well in body and in mind. They said Jesus filled people with peace, with love, and with caring, making them feel as if they were once again being held in the protective warmth of their mothers' arms.

The young man was intrigued by the love that seemed to flow from Jesus, and he reached out to touch him. Jesus turned when he felt his touch and asked, "Why did you touch me?"

"Because I want to be close to you, Master."

"It is not necessary to touch me for that to occur," Jesus responded.

"Oh, but it is," the young man said. "If I touch you, I'll know you're just like us. You make me feel so good. I feel like I'm floating. I feel peace, comfort, and warmth."

Tears began to fall from his eyes, and he said: "Master, when you are gone, who will make us feel this good? Will you be forgotten? How will people get to know you? Will it be by word of mouth? The truth about you can change over the years, can't it?"

Jesus smiled at the young man, extended his arms, reached out, and hugged him. Then he said: "My son, many will come after me and continue what I am doing. They will tell people about my love and my Father's love. In time they will repeat my words and explain my death."

The young man pulled away from Jesus and said in a high-pitched, troubled voice, "Master, Master."

"Quiet," Jesus said.

"Will you not die of old age?" the man asked.

Jesus smiled again and said: "My friend, I would like to die of old age, but I know in my heart and from what has been told me that I must suffer much pain and sorrow. I do not dwell on these thoughts because I know my Father is just and will care for me."

The young man returned to Jesus' arms. Jesus held him like a child and said, "Don't ever be frightened, for I will always be there when you call me."

A Heart Filleð with Love anð Hate

Jesus sat among his followers. As they talked, a young man came and sat among them. John said, "Shall I tell him to leave, Peter?" Peter shook his head and said: "You know how the Master is. What we say is for all ears to hear."

John nodded because he knew Peter was correct.

Jesus continued as his followers questioned him about many topics. A young man said: "Master, I have heard much about your wisdom and that you are a wise and honest man, that you speak about issues that others are afraid to address. Much tragedy has befallen me; my two sons were taken from their grandfather's house and killed. My heart has been heavy ever since. I have taken other children into my house, and I have been good to them—those who have no family or who have families that do not care for them. But my heart is heavy, Master, and many times I have asked why this happened."

Jesus rose, placed his hands on the young man's shoulders, and said, "There is much compassion and caring in your heart. When your own sons were taken from you, you filled your home with others. There is love in you, but there is also hate. You have tried to take this hurt away. You have given but not fully."

Then Jesus looked down at the earth and said: "When a mother loses her child, there always remains a place in her heart. That child is not forgotten. When a man loses his riches, he sometimes longs for what he could have had. As we grow older, we long for youth, and when we are young, we long for wisdom and strength. It seems that throughout our lifetime we always long for something we have either lost or never had."

Jesus hesitated and then said: "The earth will be here for many years, many years. But we are here for a short time. We are here to grow, to teach and to understand." Then he looked directly at the young man once again and said: "It is good to speak with friends who comfort and understand you. But it is you and you alone who has the heavy heart. Do not let it continue to harbor hatred and bitterness. Wash it with your tears and make it clean."

Then he said to the young man, "Peace, my son, peace." A tear formed in Jesus' eye because his heart was heavy. He knew what the young man felt.

The Holy Family

Mary and Joseph Are Thrilled at Jesus' Birth

Joseph sat, staring at the child. "Why do you stare, Joseph?" Mary asked. "You look as though you have never seen a child before. Come, hold your son and sing to him."

Joseph laughed and said, "Mary, a man does not sing to his child, especially a male child."

Mary replied, "But he is special."

"Special in what way?" Joseph asked. "He eats like any other child and soils like any other child."

Mary laughed and said, "But he is special."

Joseph put his hand on Mary and said: "Yes, he is. He is not my child, but I accept him as my child. What do you think, Mary? Why has this happened? Have you ever wondered about it?"

"Yes," Mary said, "many times. When I carried him, I was very concerned. As my body grew, I felt guilty because he was not your child."

Joseph said: "At times, I also wondered. But now that he is here, I am pleased."

"Weren't you pleased when I carried the child?" Mary asked.

"In many ways I was not. But when other men teased me because we are so different in age, it made me feel good."

Mary said: "Joseph, it doesn't matter. I love you."

"I love you too," he said. "And I know I'm going to love this child. I feel good about this child—and a son at that."

"Yes," Mary said, "but we knew it would be a male child."

"What do you think he's going to do?" Joseph asked.

"You've asked that before," Mary answered. "I don't know, but I only hope and pray that everyone will be pleased by his birth."

With pride in his eyes, Joseph said: "And they will think he is my son."

Mary began to laugh and said: "Yes, the carpenter's son."

He sighed and said: "Yes. Maybe he will build a new temple."

Mary said: "No. I think there is something a little more special for him to do."

"What could be more special than building the temple?" Joseph asked. "There's something very special about this child,"

"Look, Joseph, look," Mary said. The child seemed to laugh.

"He is smiling at us," Joseph exclaimed.

Mary smiled back at Joseph and said: "I don't think he really sees us, my husband; I don't think he really sees us. But whatever, we will try to be good, loving, and caring parents. You shall teach him your trade, and I shall teach him to make bread and fetch water from the well."

Then, all at once, a shiver seemed to run through Joseph and he said: "Mary, do you realize that this truly is a special child? He was given to us for a reason. What burden lies on our shoulders? What are we to do? We cannot tell anyone. What are we to do?"

Mary said: "In time we will know. I hope and pray that he does not break my heart."

"My prayer exactly," Joseph said, "my prayer exactly."

No Room in the Inn

The crowd at the inn was very noisy. Joseph was somewhat frightened at the way people were pushing and shoving one another. He entered the door to the inn and made his way through the crowd to a woman who was serving broth and bread. He said to her, "I would like some of both."

"Shut up," a man nearby said to him. "I was here before you."

The shoving and pushing continued, the stench was overpowering, but Joseph was determined to stay because Mary needed nourishment. She had eaten the last piece of bread, and Joseph knew Mary needed to be strengthened by some food if she was to continue nursing her newborn son.

He turned toward another man who was calling out: "I'm hungry. I'm hungry. Broth for the weary traveler."

Joseph said, "My wife has given birth to a son."

The man looked at him and said, "What did you say?"

Joseph said again: "My wife has given birth to a son. She is hungry, and I must get her some of this broth and bread."

The woman who was pouring the broth into the bowls called out: "The broth and bread are only for those staying at the inn. You are not staying in the inn. You are not staying here. Get out."

The man Joseph spoke to looked at the woman and said, "I'll share my bread and broth with him because his wife has just given birth."

The woman cackled as she handed the food to him, and Joseph and the man worked their way out of the large room. Joseph was grateful for the man's kindness and generosity. He was much younger than Joseph, and Joseph did not know if the man obtained the food because his voice was strong or because he had slipped an extra coin to the woman.

The two of them entered the cave where Mary and her child lay. Even the animals appeared to be attentive to them. Joseph said proudly, "This is my wife and child."

Mary began to rise, but the man quickly said to her: "Do not get up. I wish only to see the child. Rest. I am sure you are tired."

Mary slowly and carefully removed the veil covering Jesus' face. "This is my son, our son," she said.

The man asked at what time the child had been born. After Joseph told him, the man got up and walked away, saying: "I will be back."

Mary really enjoyed the hot broth and the fresh bread. When the man returned, he had bread, oil, and wine in his hands. "This," he said, "is a gift from me to you. But I shall also give you anther gift. I tell you this: Your son shall be well known throughout the world." Joseph looked at Mary as the man continued speaking: "Woman, woman, there was fear in you when you conceived this child, fear, when you brought him into this world; and there will be even more fear when he leaves your arms and begins his journey through this life. You have brought forth a son, a son whom they shall acclaim as the mighty one. His words shall be filled with strength, and his deeds with kindness and caring."

He looked down at the child's hands, stroked them slowly, and said: "These are healing hands. He was born under the sign of an important and revealing star. Many have waited for this child." He looked at Joseph and said: "My friend, I do not know you, and you do not know me. But what I tell you now repeat to no one else. Do not stay here too long, for your child must live."

Then he looked at Mary and said: "Woman, woman, remember my words. Your tears will be many, but without this child there would be no hope for humankind."

Joseph said, "How do you know this?"

The man answered: "I have read it in the stars, and I have seen it in his hands and face. I have not come this way by chance. I was led here. I was led by the message of the stars."

He looked at Joseph and said: "My friend, when I saw you in the crowd, I was drawn to you. I did not know at first what you were saying. But when I heard you say, 'My wife has given birth,' I knew that if you believed in dreams, you would know that what I have told you is true.

Joseph nodded: "Before the birth of my son, I dreamed a man would come and give us broth, oil, and bread, that there would be no room in the inn, and that those who provided for us would judge us not."

Tears began to roll slowly from the man's eyes and to fall on his sun-baked, weathered face. He said: "Peace, my friends, peace. Do not forget my words and remember that he is never yours alone. He is for all of humankind."

Hurting Those We Love Most

When Mary entered the house, her face was red and swollen from shedding many tears. "Joseph, my husband," she sobbed, "our neighbor Zachery is such a cruel man. His wife cried out in pain while giving birth to a fine, healthy son, and all he did was curse her."

Joseph put down the board he was working on and said, "I can't believe it."

"It's true," Mary said. "It's true."

Joseph said: "How fortunate he is. This is his fifth son, isn't it?"

"Yes," Mary answered, and then she looked at Jesus who lay fast asleep. "We have only one son, Joseph, but we truly have been blessed."

"Yes," Joseph smiled proudly. "He is strong and healthy."

Mary picked Jesus up and cuddled him in her arms, rocking him back and forth. She said, "For three years we have had this gift."

Joseph, mumbling, almost talking to himself, said, "and Zachery cursed his son."

"Maybe I'm too harsh on him," Mary said. "You know he's been troubled since the uncle he worked with died. He's not a good businessman. Perhaps he's worried he won't be able to provide for his family with the addition of a new son."

Joseph said: "I have known him for a long time, even before he took a wife, and he was never like this. He was very proud every time his wife gave birth."

Joseph looked at Jesus and said: "Mary, during the time you carried him, there were times I thought I would not be able to love him. For I knew . . . " He quickly stopped.

"That he was not yours," Mary said.

Joseph looked down in shame and embarrassment and said, "Mary, it is wrong to hold hatred in the heart and in the mind, is it not?"

"Yes," Mary said. "I felt shame at times but could not tell you."

Spontaneously, without words, they embraced, with Mary still holding Jesus in her arms. The three of them were one in love. Joseph kissed Mary on the cheek and said rhetorically, "When we are troubled, why do we hurt those we love the most—sometimes even our own children who are gifts of our love to one another?"

Mary looked at Jesus and said, "Yes, in our old age he will give us great joy."

A Child Is a Mother's Child Forever

*M*ary looked with great love in her eyes at her sleeping child and gently wiped the beads of perspiration from his forehead. His hair was damp and covered with tight curls. Joseph watched while she took her finger and curled his hair around it. "Mary, Mary," he said, "you won't be able to do that much longer, for he will grow older and object."

Mary looked at Joseph and said: "Shame on you. Do you not understand that a child is a child to his mother forever? No matter how old a child becomes, he remains his mother's child."

Joseph smiled: "My mother told me the same thing when I was young, before she died. Mothers are all alike, aren't they?"

Mary smiled, sort of giggled, and said: "In some ways, I guess we are. For when you bear a child, you want only the very best for him, and that's why you get angry at him at times. When your child leaves home, you forget those times. You want him to be able to stand alone and grow, but it stings and hurts your heart. And before long, you need him to help you; you become the child, and he the adult.

"I tell you this, Joseph: There is great wisdom in the Father's rules. We all enter this world as babes to suck at our mother's breast, to be taught, to learn to stand on our own feet, to leave home, and to return there. Is this not what happens, Joseph? And then when it is time, we close our eyes, our bodies rest in the sleep of death, and we are reunited with the Father, our Creator."

Mary and Joseph Take Jesus to the Temple

Mary was very tired because she had not slept well the night before, but she knew the time had come to take Jesus to the temple. Joseph looked lovingly at Jesus, who was a beautiful baby. He picked him up and held him close to his heart. Mary watched with half-opened eyes as she fought sleep.

Joseph carried Jesus to the door as they prepared to leave and said: "We are going to make a journey now, my son, so that you may be blessed. You will be blessed." Mary quickly wiped Jesus' face before they began their journey. When they arrived at the temple, they were greeted by many people. Joseph was more than just proud as he showed off his son to everyone.

An old woman approached them, looked deeply into Mary's tired eyes, and then looked at Jesus. When the old woman began to weep, Mary asked: "Why do you weep? Why do you weep when you look at my child?"

The old woman asked Joseph if she could hold the child, and Joseph reluctantly gave Jesus to her. She held him to her bosom while her tears fell on him. Jesus began to stir, and then he too began to cry.

Mary reached out to take him, but the old woman took two steps back, still holding him firmly to her chest. Looking at Jesus, the old woman said, "My child, my child, what I see brings tears to my eyes even though you are a gift to all the people of the world, even those not yet born."

Mary looked at Joseph with fear in her eyes and once again reached for her child, but the old woman still held Jesus tightly. She said to Mary: "Your tears will be many, my child. Your tears will be many. You cried at his birth, but you shall weep and cry out at his death."

Mary became angry. You could see it in her face, and she said, "Old woman, old woman, why do you say such things to me?"

Still clutching the child, the old woman raised her hand, placed it on Mary's lips, and said: "Silence, mother, silence. What I am telling you, you already know in your heart."

Joseph was stunned. She turned to him and said: "You are not the father of this child. This child belongs to the world." Then, reluctantly, she handed the child to Mary.

With tears in his eyes a high priest who was standing and listening in the background slowly approached Jesus, Mary, and Joseph and said: "The old woman speaks the truth. Come. It is time."

Jesus Is a Special Gift

When Jesus was still very young, he said to his mother, "Is the lamb my brother?"

Mary laughed and said, "My son, my son, why do you ask such a question?"

"Well, you told me I should be good to my lamb, that I should give it water, and that I should show it love."

"The lamb is a gift," Mary said, "a gift and a source of hope."

"Of hope?" Jesus wondered aloud.

"Yes," Mary said, "for the lamb speaks in its own way and is able to show you it likes you, does it not?"

"Yes," Jesus answered. "But, Mother, do you think the Father loves me or the lamb more?"

"You, of course, my son, for you are his gift to me and to your Father and to the world. Do you not understand that we are all gifts?"

"My lamb, too?" Jesus asked.

"He is a gift, too, but in a different way. He is a gift to you as we are all gifts to the Father because we are a source of pride to him, and as the Father is a gift to us because he protects and guides us."

Jesus said, "Mother, you speak in ways I do not understand."

Mary smiled and said as she bent down and kissed his hot and sweaty forehead: "My son, my son, you are my gift, and we are the Father's gifts. He didn't want people to be lonely, and so he gave us animals to talk to us in their own way and to be companions to us. We are to care for them and work together with them."

Jesus said, "Mother, the Father must really love us."

"Yes," Mary said. "He has given us the earth to grow food, trees with fruit to eat and branches to keep us warm and to bake the bread. He has given us hay and wheat so we can feed ourselves and the animals. When we care for the animals and work with them, we also work with the Father, who has created them. Some people are unable to become close to others, but they may possess a special ability to care for the animals."

"Is this wrong, Mother?"

"No, it's not wrong," Mary answered, "for we are all different. The grains of wheat look alike until you put them on top of one another and discover there are slight differences among them. That is how the Father has made each of us."

Jesus never forgot how his mother held him close and said, "You are my special gift from the Father, and I must share you with everyone." And he remembered her gentle kiss and the warmth of her hug as she held him tight in her arms.

Why Are There Stars

Jesus said to his mother with joy and excitement in his voice: "Please, Mother, please. Come out and watch with me."

"Watch what, my son?" Mary asked. "The darkness of night already covers us."

"Please?"

Mary couldn't say no to him, so she went outside with her son. "You'll be cold out here," she said as she wrapped her arms around him and held him. He snuggled close, and love flowed back and forth between them, warming their hearts.

"Mother, I have a question," Jesus said.

"Only one?" she smiled. "You usually have many. What do you want to know, my son. I will try to answer if I can."

Jesus hesitated only briefly, forming the question in his mind, and then asked, "Why are there lights in the sky?"

Mary looked at the stars for a long time before she said, "Maybe the Father wishes us to know that he's always there."

"But, Mother, " Jesus said, "the stars sometimes hide behind the clouds."

"That's true," Mary said as she thought about it and searched for an answer that might satisfy her son's curiosity. "I asked my mother the same question when I was young, and she told me the stars are windows to the heavens through which our heavenly Father sheds his tears when he is sad. What do you think about the stars, son?"

"I'm not sure, Mother, but I enjoy looking at them. Sometimes I imagine them to be twinkling embers. They comfort me like raindrops. They're like a blanket to protect us and keep us warm."

Just then Joseph joined them and joined Mary in putting his arms around his son.

Jesus asked him, "Father, what do the stars tell us?"

"I can only tell you this, my son: When you were born, I saw a beautiful, beautiful star. It told me your mother's time was near."

Jesus looked puzzled and said, "Father, I don't understand."

Joseph and Mary shared a knowing look, and Joseph said: "I remember well how my heart overflowed with joy when you were born. I felt like the richest man on earth. No one could have given me a greater gift. I could tell from your cry, from the sound of new life, that you were a boy."

"Yes," Mary said, "like the star we saw in the heavens and claimed as our own, you have entered our life and kept it warm and beautiful."

They hugged each other, held hands, and Jesus said: "I'm glad the three of us are together. I'm filled with so much love."

"And so are we," Joseph and Mary said in unison.

All three looked up at the sky, no one saying it, but each searching for that special star. After a while Jesus asked, "Mother, what will I be when I grow up?"

Joseph answered quickly and proudly, "A carpenter."

Then Mary answered gently and with great feeling, "A father."

Jesus kept looking at the stars and said, "I think I shall be both—a builder and a father of many."

They watched the stars together prayerfully, and their love was very strong that night.

All Women Are Blessed

*J*esus was about ten years old as he walked along the road with his mother. Mary stopped and said, "Son, let's rest for a while." Jesus was eager to get home, but he sat obediently with his mother. She said, "Do you see what I see?"

Jesus looked all around, his eyes darting here and there. Finally, he gave up and asked, "What, Mother?"

She smiled her usual gentle smile and answered: "The flower, my son. It's a gift from the Father."

"Oh, yes, Mother, I see it."

Mary touched it gently so that it would not break.

"Why don't you pick it?" Jesus asked.

"And destroy its beauty?" Mary quickly responded. "It should be seen and enjoyed by all." Mary stared at the flower and seemed to be lost in thought.

"What are you thinking, Mother?" Jesus asked.

"When I was a child," Mary said, "I too walked this road with my favorite aunt who taught me much. She never had any children, but her understanding of them and her love for them were very great. I believe it was on this very spot that she and I sat down together, and she told me about the Father," Mary said, her eyes looking down at the earth first and then up at the heavens. "She told me how much she loved him, that even though she didn't have any children, there was much love in her heart because she was a woman, and she believed all women are blessed by the Father in a special way. She told me some of her neighbors thought she had been cursed because she hadn't brought any children into the world. But she wasn't frightened, because she knew this wasn't true; while mothers were busy carrying out their many responsibilities, she was able to spend more time meditating on God's many gifts and caring for the children who had no parents and no one to love them.

"She believed she could help people to recognize God's gifts through the seeds of love she planted in them through her sharing with them and caring for them, as she did with me. God's gifts are to be seen and enjoyed by all. All of life is a gift—your life, my life, your father's life, the lives of those who are our friends and those who are not, even this small but beautiful flower. It is in teaching truths like these to the young that good will overcome evil."

Jesus looked down at the flower and asked, "Who planted the seed, Mother?"

Mary smiled again, "Have I talked to you in vain, my son?"

He smiled back knowingly at her, kissed her, and said, "You loved your aunt very much, Mother, didn't you?"

"Yes," she said, "and I still do. She is a part of me. She had no children, but she gave me great joy in sharing God's love with me, as this flower does with us now."

Jesus Delivers Bread

Jesus said to his mother: "I'm tired. Why do I have to take the bread now? It's such a long walk to the other side of town."

Mary smiled and said: "My son, did not the Father give you two good feet to walk and run, and a strong back and hands?"

Jesus smiled back and said: "But my friends are going to the marketplace, and I want to go with them."

Mary said: "But I know a family who has very little to eat, and I want you to take them some of my freshly baked bread."

"Why me?" Jesus asked.

"Why not?" Mary said.

"But mother . . . " Jesus argued.

Joseph was about to intervene, but Mary looked at him in a way that let him know she had everything under control.

Jesus asked, "Mother, why should you give them bread?"

"Because we have been blessed with food and should share it," Mary answered. "We have no extra coins to give, but we can share our love with this bread."

Not quite convinced, Jesus placed the loaves of bread in a cloth sack and started his walk to the other side of town. On the way he kicked a stone, watched a fight, heard women gossiping at the well, and stared at the Roman soldiers. He wasn't in any real hurry.

It was dark by the time he reached the home where his mother had told him to deliver the bread. The man extended his arms in gratitude and exclaimed, "My son, you have brought us something to eat."

When the man and his little children began to hug him, Jesus felt guilty and said: "I must tell you. I didn't want to bring the bread today."

The man, who looked very tired, his face dirty from working in the fields, said: "I understand. My wife has died, and I still miss her so much. At times I don't feel like going to work, but I must provide for my family. It is late, and it is dangerous to walk about. Spend the night with us," he urged Jesus.

"My mother will worry," Jesus said.

"She'll worry more if she thinks you're trying to find your way home at night."

So Jesus stayed.

When he awoke, the man was gone and the children were playing. Their eyes strayed often to the last piece of bread. Jesus was hungry, but he knew he was not nearly as hungry as they were. So he gave them the bread, went to the well, brought back some water, and wiped them clean while they laughed gleefully. The smallest child snuggled close to him and tears began to fall from her eyes.

"You miss your mother, don't you?" Jesus asked her.

She was too young to answer, but an older child answered, "Our Father said we must be strong, but your mother's kindness makes me sad because it reminds me of my mother."

"My Father provides for those in need when we share his love," Jesus said. "You must care for your brothers and sisters."

When Jesus returned home, he hugged and kissed his mother before she could express her anger at his not coming home. "Mother, I love you. I'm glad I still have you, and I'm sorry I complained yesterday," Jesus said quickly and with great sincerity.

Mary's anger melted.

"The Father will always provide for us, won't he, Mother?" "Yes," Mary said, "both your father and the Father we do not see. A father may not provide his children with coin, but the Father always offers us his love."

Mary Is a Gift of Joy

Mary began to cry. Through her tears she said: "I've ruined it. The bread is as hard as a stone."

Joseph heard her, came into the house, and said: "Why are you weeping? Are they tears of love or tears of sadness falling upon the bread?"

Mary motioned as if she were going to throw the bread, but she stopped and started crying even harder.

Joseph put his arms around her and said: "Woman, woman, you mean you've never made a mistake before?"

"I've made many," Mary said.

"Am I one of them?" Joseph asked with a smile.

She looked at him and together they began to laugh. "You are a gift," Mary said to Joseph.

"No," Joseph said, "you are the gift, for you have been my comfort and warmth."

Jesus entered the house and called out, "Mother, Father." They extended their arms to their son, and Joseph said, "My son, your mother has baked bread."

Jesus picked it up and said, "Father, it is as hard as a rock."

"But this is one rock we shall enjoy," Joseph said, and he and Mary smiled.

"Soak it in some milk, and maybe it will be fine," Jesus suggested.

"Yes, let's do that," Joseph agreed.

Mary shook her head and said, "Not even the goat's milk will soften this bread."

"Then we shall give it away," Jesus said.

"No," Mary responded, "we don't give away our mistakes as if they were gifts. We give only what is good and pleasing."

Jesus said, "Mother, you have been both laughing and crying."

Mary looked at her son, her only son, and said: "My child, that is part of being a woman, and I am glad to be a woman because it has given me the greatest of gifts—it has given me you."

Joseph nodded in agreement and said, "You have been a gift of joy to me also."

"Not all women are blessed with children," Mary said. "Some are barren, and others have no man to lie at their side. But all women are blessed in being created to be the bearers of life."

Jesus Feels Compassion and Fear

Jesus was helping his mother knead bread dough. He commented, "Mother, I enjoy working with you."

Joseph smiled and asked, "And what about me, my son?"

Jesus smiled back at him and answered, "O yes, I enjoy working with you too, Father, but I also like getting my hands into dough."

"It can be a chore though if you have to do it every day," Mary said.

Jesus kissed his mother and said, "I better go and help my father."

"But you are not finished yet," Mary objected mildly.

Jesus looked at her and, thinking very quickly, said, "True, Mother, but you do it so much better than I do."

Mary shook her head, laughed, and thought to herself: "He has such a special place in my heart. I wish he'd stay with me and never grow up." But she knew that couldn't be and a strange sadness filled her heart when she heard Jesus laughing with Joseph.

When the bread had been baked, Mary called out, "My son, my son, come and help me. We have a journey to make."

Joseph said to her, "You are a good woman for doing this, Mary."

"My husband," she responded, "we could not do this if it were not for you."

"We work together as family," Joseph said.

Jesus asked, "Where are we going, Mother?"

Mary answered, "You'll see, my son, you'll see."

Then she carefully wrapped the round, flat loaves in a clean cloth and said, "Joseph, may I have some of the goat's milk to take with us?"

Joseph responded, "But there's only enough for us."

"We can drink water," Mary said and seemed to be happy as she filled a skin with the milk.

The journey was long, and Jesus grew tired and hungry.

Suddenly Mary stopped and asked, "Do you hear voices, my son?"

Jesus answered: "Yes, Mother. I hear both wailing and laughter."

"It is the unclean," Mary said. "They live nearby."

Jesus wanted to run, but Mary put her hand on his shoulder and said, "Don't be afraid, my son; we won't get too close."

Mary called out, "Old woman, it's Mary. Do you hear me?"

No one came forward, and so Mary said in a firm voice to Jesus, "Hold the bread and milk, sit here, and don't move."

Jesus asked, "But, Mother, what if someone comes?"

Mary responded, "Do not be afraid, my son, because I will be right here to protect you."

Mary walked forward and called out, "It's Mary."

Finally a voice called back, "Unclean, unclean, unclean."

Again Mary said, "It's Mary. I have my son with me, and we have brought you bread."

Jesus looked with amazement at a man who looked hideous, and then at a young girl about his age who clung to the man's side.

With tears in her eyes, the girl asked Jesus, "Have you come to play with me?"

"No," her father answered. "We are unclean."

Jesus felt fear and compassion at the same time and looked into his mother's eyes to know what to do. She shook her head—no.

Mary said, "We have brought you some bread and all the milk we have in case there is a child who needs it."

The father said to his little girl, "See, there is good in people. Some bring us food they have made with their own hands, and others throw us scraps, but they do it with love."

The man looked at Jesus and said, "Your mother is a good woman to have made such a long journey to bring us food."

The morning after they had returned home Jesus asked his mother, "Why did we have to go to such a place?"

Mary answered, "My son, the heart as well as the mind must learn many important lessons in life—the love one learns in giving to the poor is one of those necessary lessons."

A Home Needs a Mother and a Father

Jesus seemed to be lost in thought at the doorway of his home. His mother approached him and asked gently, "Son, to what far-off places has your mind carried you?"

Jesus did not answer.

Again Mary asked in her soft and gentle voice, "Son, is something troubling you?"

Jesus still did not respond.

Joseph called out, "Son, your mother is speaking to you."

As if he had heard a magic bell ring in his ears, Jesus looked up and asked, "Father, did you say something?"

Mary and Joseph answered his question by smiling at one another, knowing that a mother's voice does not always bring the immediate response that a father's does.

Mary placed her arms around Jesus and asked, "Why don't you tell me what you're thinking about?"

Jesus looked at his mother and said, "You may think it's a foolish thought, but I can't understand why God gives two to each child."

Mary didn't know what he meant at first, but she asked intuitively, "You mean a mother and a father?"

"Yes," Jesus replied.

Mary explained, "The mother brings life into the world, and the father cares for that life by sharing his wisdom and strength with that child."

Jesus looked down at the ground and said with some hesitation in his voice, "I love both of you, but why couldn't one do what two do?"

Mary quickly searched her mind, as she often had to do when her son asked his many questions, and said: "Does not the coin have two sides? Is there not both light and darkness?"

"Yes, Mother," Jesus said. "Are you telling me that it is with wisdom that our heavenly Father created?"

Mary answered, "Yes." Then she explained further: "The mother bears the gift of life from God, but without the father she could not give it to the world. Both mother and father reflect the image of our God, who is strength and understanding on one side, and love and compassion on the other."

Joseph had been listening intently, and he spoke out: "I tell you this, my son: A home cannot be a home when either is missing. Mother and father, husband and wife, give their love and strength one to the other until each of them is able to give both."

"Yes," Mary broke in, "like the night becomes the day, and the day becomes the night."

Jesus thought for a while and then said, "I think I understand, but I'm not sure."

Joseph said: "Look at it this way. We cannot live on bread alone or on water alone. We need both. Perhaps only the Father knows why for sure, but in his hidden wisdom he has ordered that life enter the world through a mother and a father."

Jesus Dreams about Crucifixion

Jesus came to his mother's side as she was still waking from sleep, crawled in between her and Joseph, and said, "Mother, I keep dreaming the same dream."

Mary smiled at Joseph and said, "Was it a good dream, my son?"

"I am not sure, Mother," Jesus answered.

"Well then, why don't you tell us about it," Joseph said.

Jesus looked up, as if into the heavens, and started to describe his dream as best as he could remember it: "I was standing all by myself in a large house that had many, many doors and many, many windows. But all of a sudden, when I looked again, men and women and children were staring at me through the windows and doors. Then they started yelling."

Mary looked with some concern at Joseph, not liking the fright in Jesus' voice and in his eyes, and asked, "My child, did they say anything to you?"

"Mother," Jesus said, "they shouted 'crucify him, crucify him.'" Jesus began to cry, and Mary took him into her arms and gave him all the love she could. Through his tears Jesus said, "Mother, some cried for my flesh and blood, some said they loved me, and some said nothing."

Mary began to weep and said softly, "Remove this dream from your mind, my son." But Mary knew this dream would remain in her heart forever with other dreams that had already come true. And she hoped—as only a mother can when she is worried about one of her children—that this dream would not come true.

Jesus Remembers His Childhood

Jesus Visits His Mother Unannounced

Jesus came home unannounced to visit his mother. He had been away for a while and came alone. As he drew near, he stopped and looked at the house where he was raised, where his mother and father had cared for him and loved him. A mixture of sadness and joy welled up within his heart at the same time. It seemed so long since he was a child. He longed to return to those days when life was much simpler and happier. His eyes caught sight of his mother as she sat crushing the grains of wheat to make bread. She didn't see her son and seemed to be unaware of the many noises coming from the street.

Jesus looked up into the pure blue sky where there was peace and contentment, and then down at the street filled with filth and human suffering—one child calling out for his mother, another child crying in hunger, an old man struggling to carry a heavy jar of water. When he entered the house, joy filled Mary's heart, showing through her eyes, and the warmth of love stronger than the sun filled her whole being as Jesus hugged and kissed her.

"Mother," he said.

"My son, my son, my son," Mary repeated.

They sat down together and began to tell each other what they had been doing. As they shared the bread she had baked earlier, he noticed she was growing old and tired. Gentle lines were appearing on her face.

"What are you staring at, son?" she asked.

"At you, Mother."

"Haven't you looked at me before?" she asked.

"Yes, Mother, but I am seeing you in a new light now that I am grown."

"Is it a good light or a bad light, my son?" she asked, laughing.

"Mother, you are making fun, and I am serious. I see you as I have never seen you before. I spend many nights alone now, thinking of how you loved and cared for me and so many of our friends. When I was hurt in body or spirit, you comforted me. When I was cold, you warmed me with your body by drawing me close to you. When

I was frightened, you held me tight and wiped my tears away with your cloak. There were also times when we got angry at each other, and oh, how I remember that look of yours, that disapproving look. Sometimes I find myself looking at people that way. I also remember how silent you became at times and would not talk to anyone. That both hurt and angered me, but I soon realized you were teaching me an important lesson. And so when I pray to the heavenly Father and ask for an answer but get only silence, I am able to bear the frustration better. I also remember the many times you held me for no reason at all and poured out your love on me. A mother's love is so special, shared already with the child in the womb."

Mary didn't move. Even her eyelashes didn't flicker.

"Woman, woman," Jesus said, "you are special not only in my eyes, but in the eyes of all men women, and children, in the eyes of my Father, and in the heavens. You are a source of comfort to hold us in our joy or sorrow, in life and in death. You shall never be forgotten, for truly you are the mother of us all."

Only then did Mary begin to speak, "But I am only the mother of . . . "

"Do not speak, Mother. Many times silence is a gift. I know I have been given to you, and the time will come when you will be given to the world."

Love Remains in the Heart

A group of men who were tired, worn, and hungry gathered to listen to Jesus. A sense of peace seemed to cover them as they huddled near a small fire and spoke quietly to one another. Jesus said to them, "I can feel the peace within you, and so it is a good night to talk about whatever is in your hearts and minds." The men agreed with him.

As they shared the bread they had, they began to speak about their childhood years. A young man by the name of Joseph said: "I have followed you now through three cities. You have talked about many things but never about your parents."

Jesus nodded and agreed with him.

The young man asked, "Did your mother ever tell you anything about your birth?"

Jesus looked strangely at him and said, "Why do you ask such a question?"

The young man replied: "I was found at the city gates and was kept. My mother was a good woman. She was a beggar who had children of her own, but she took me in and cared for me in the same way that she did her own children. I was accepted and loved by her."

Jesus sighed and said: "She was a good woman, as my mother is. My mother has never said much to me about my birth except that there was great joy in her heart along with sadness. My father would never say anything when she talked about my birth. He would only turn away. But when he was dying, he said to me: 'My son, my son, I am old and tired, and soon I must leave, but I want you to remember that your mother, the woman who gave you birth, is very special. She has been a good, kind, and just mother to you. She has taught you well.' Then he looked down at his hands and said, 'I have worked many years with you. My father was a carpenter, and I followed in his footsteps. But you, my son, have greater things to do—a mission beyond words.' Then he gasped and took his last breath."

After a brief pause Jesus continued: "My mother began to weep. We held one another, knowing his time had come. My mother looked at me with tears in her eyes and said: 'Son, you were a beautiful gift given to us, but I know you will leave me in time. When you do, remember that you were loved and you will always be loved. People may hurt you with words that will sting, but remember that you are special, special in the eyes of the heavenly Father. You are his Son, and we are only instruments of his love to guide you. The man who now lies in deep sleep loved you like no other human father could love you.' Then she gently wiped the tears from her eyes and spread them on my cheek. I shall never forget her gentleness and the warmth of her tears."

Then Jesus looked down at the fire, began to stoke it, and said: "Her love is like this fire. In time it will go out, and she will join my father, but her love will always remain warm and strong within my heart."

Jesus Worries about His Mother

*T*had been a very long and tiring day for Jesus and his followers. Many people had come to him, hoping to be healed in body or mind. Some came only to see the man called Jesus of Nazareth, the master, the healer.

When night had fallen, Jesus sat with his small band of friends, including Peter, Andrew, and John. They all seemed to be lost in thought when Jesus got up slowly and began to walk away. No one saw it, but tears fell from his eyes. Only nature heard the sob that escaped from his throat. He was feeling lonely and longed to see his mother.

As he walked, he noticed a tiny, pulsating light near the trees. As he drew closer to it, the light grew brighter. Jesus asked: "Who comes? Who has the light?"

No one answered. There was no sound.

And so, Jesus asked again, "Who comes?"

There was a response this time. It sounded like a voice within a voice—a voice and yet not a voice.

Time seemed to stand still for a while before the voice was heard again, saying: "Do not be sorrowful, my son. I know you miss your earthly family. Your mother pines too, for she worries about you so much. Be strengthened, my son, for you have much to do in my name." The light continued to shine, but the voice said nothing more.

Jesus turned and walked back to the small group of men who were sleeping around the fire. He lay down and thought about his mother. He was worried about her because he knew how difficult it was for her to be living in his hometown. People who did not believe in him mocked and scorned her. They would say, "What can you expect from a carpenter's son—a healer?"

Jesus knew, however, that his mother would only smile and respond, "From a weed can come a flower." Then she would turn and walk away without saying anything else.

Jesus looked up at the sky and prayed that one day he might see his mother in the light of the sun and that others might also.

Mary Tells Jesus about His Birth

he disciples sat around a fire telling stories about their youth. Judas said, "Master, you have not told us a story about when you were young.

Jesus smiled and responded: "I remember some of the words my mother spoke to me. They have been gifts to me.

"When I was but a child, I sat by her feet while she spun wool. She had tears in her eyes but a smile on her face. I asked her, 'Mother, why do you have such a strange look on your face?' She told me about an angel that came to her when she was very young. I asked her, 'What is an angel?'

"She responded with a very beautiful smile—a smile I shall forever keep in my mind. She told me that this angel spoke to her and that she agreed to the Father's request of her.

"Mother said nothing else as the years passed. And then one day as she was drawing water at the well and I came to help her, she had the same strange look on her face. She was smiling with tears in her eyes. Once again I asked why. She replied, 'My son, while I was drawing water I heard the most beautiful voice. It said, "My child, be not fearful, for soon he will leave, but you will never be forgotten."' She said nothing more. I have often thought about these words. They give me comfort because I know I am doing the Father's will."

Peter asked, "But Master, how did you know that you must do the Father's will?"

Again Jesus smiled and replied: "Before I gathered all of you, my mother and I sat for a long time in silence and then with tears in her eyes and sadness on her face she handed me the bread she had baked, a bit of oil, and some salt. She said: 'My son, my son, I give this to you. My home, our home, is always open. But I know now that you must go to do the Father's will.' She hugged me and continued, 'Now my son, go in peace and may all my prayers for you be answered.' I did not turn. I could not. But I knew in my heart that she loved me, would always love me and would be there when my time came."

Each Family Is an Important Gift

While Jesus stood by an olive tree, he reached out and gently touched the bark with his hand. Peter watched him and said: "Master, why do you love nature so much? When you teach us various truths, such as the Father's love for us, you frequently refer to the earth, the sea, and the sky, to stones and trees and birds."

Jesus smiled at Peter and said: "These are all gifts given by my Father to humans. People return his gifts and give great joy to the Father when there is caring, unity, and love in the family because of the way in which people have used them."

"Are not caring and love the same thing?" one of his disciples asked.

"No," Jesus answered. "Each of them is a separate gift—in the same way that water is a gift to the earth and the tree is a gift to humanity. Each family is also an important gift, for it is there that each of us grows and learns how to give and to receive. Sharing our gifts with others is as important as receiving them. My mother's love was a beautiful gift to me. She gave it freely and fully. I cannot say that she has never reprimanded me or that she has always agreed with what I have said and done, but I can say that she has never withheld her love from me. The love of a mother in her caring is as important as the love a father gives in providing for his family. The respect a father receives in being able to do this is important, and this is the way it should be if the family is to receive . . . "

"To receive what?" one of his disciples asked before Jesus had a chance to finish.

Jesus said: "I tell you this: Without a seed from which it could grow, this tree would not be here. Without a man's seed the soul could not be given to a woman by my Father and there would be no life for us to care for and to love." Then Jesus smiled, looked down at the earth, bent over, grabbed a handful of dirt and allowed it to flow slowly through his fingers. Then he said: "Man is like this dust. Earth gives life to a seed, but sometimes takes it away. Man gives life to a seed, but he also sometimes takes it away. When my time comes and I am no longer in your sight, I want you to remember my words. I want you to show my Father's love to others and to teach them about it. Tell them that they return the Father's love when they do what he wants them to do—when they care for one another and love one another."

Jesus Remembers a Fight

Mary sat, kneading and shaping the bread dough. Joseph sat, carving a piece of wood. Jesus, still a boy, said to them: "Look, there's a fight! Don't you want to watch it? Look, the Roman soldiers are just standing there and laughing. Mother! Father! Don't you hear me?"

Mary sighed, continued to knead the dough, and asked aloud, "Why can't people live together in harmony?"

Joseph answered, "Because they're like children and enjoy the excitement of fighting."

"Don't say that about children," Mary said. "They don't enjoy the sound of pain."

Joseph responded, "If men fought like children, they'd soon forget their anger and make peace, but they fight in a strange manner, almost like a wounded animal in pain."

Mary said: "Those who stand by and watch are just as guilty as those who started it. My son, keep peace in your heart and you will always be close to the Father."

Later in his life Jesus remembered this scene as he stood and watched a group of people arguing. Peter asked him: "Master, why are you staring at them?"

"Listen to them," Jesus answered. "They are arguing back and forth like children." Then, with a brief smile, he looked down at the ground and said: "Sometimes the heart becomes as hard as the stone under my foot, and the tongue never stops. It runs on and on like the stream that turns to a river and the river to a sea. Peace, peace, peace. If people could live in harmony with one another, there would be great joy in my Father's heart, and he would give many gifts to his people. But instead people act like foolish children who do not understand the Father's love and turn their back on it. What a joy it is to behold peace in a person's heart. It is the key that opens the door to my Father's home and the room where he keeps his gifts."

Mary Questions Jesus

Mary enjoyed sitting and talking alone with her son because these opportunities had become very rare. People were always coming to their house to ask him to heal sick loved ones or to ask him questions. The room was not large enough to hold all of them, and so some stood in the street. But somehow she was always able to feed them, and no one had to go away hungry. Someone always seemed to bring along extra bread.

Jesus came home unannounced this time, and so no one knew he was there. Mary felt guilty because she didn't want to tell anyone quite yet. After all, what could be wrong about wanting to spend some time with your son? Jesus smiled at her as if he knew what she was thinking, and Mary became embarrassed.

Jesus said, "I enjoy spending time like this with you."

"And I with you," Mary said. "My son, I too have questions to ask you."

"Speak them and I will try to answer them, Mother."

"Son, when you were a child, you came to me. Now I come to you."

Jesus extended his hand to his mother in a sign of deep love.

"My son, my son, will we ever truly know the Father, and will there ever be one faith in the world?"

Jesus sighed and said, "Mother, you do not ask simple questions."

"My son, I have carried them in my heart for a long time."

"Why, Mother?" Jesus asked.

"Because I believe," Mary answered. "If everyone believed as we do, there would be no problems."

Jesus smiled a half-smile and said: "There will not be complete union with my Father until the end, when humankind will no longer walk physically upon the earth. Human beings have been given a free will by my Father so that they may make their own decisions. My Father is only a guide. All people follow what they believe is the way of my Father and will never be truly united here. They are united in that everyone has a heart and a soul, but each one has a different face and a different mind."

Jesus looked more closely at his mother and said: "You are a simple woman, but you have a mind that never stops." And then he kissed her on the forehead and on the cheek where his lips felt a tear that had fallen from her eye. "Weep not," he said. "It is neither your time nor mine for tears. Be filled with joy because we can still speak freely without fear of someone wanting to hurt us for what we have said."

Jesus and Mary Thank One Another

Jesus and Mary walked together, each lost in thought. It had been a beautiful and meaningful ceremony. Mary stopped, turned, and said to her son: "I was very pleased that you came with me. Since your father's death I have felt lonely when I must be among my friends." Then Mary added quickly, "It is not that I do not enjoy their company, but family is so important when you celebrate the joy of marriage."

Jesus nodded and said, "You seemed to enjoy the food."

She nodded again and said, "And I was so pleased when they thanked those who had baked the bread and prepared the rest of the meal."

They continued to walk, and Jesus said: "The gift of life has many mysteries. What a beautiful gift the Father has given to us in the food in the fields. We can watch a seed grow to the fullness of life—a tiny seed that will bring pleasure to those who plant and care for it, for those who reap it, and for those who prepare it to be eaten."

Mary looked down at her hands and said: "For years these hands have baked bread, and each time I felt close to the heavenly Father. I always try to put in love and, yes, even hope that those who eat it will grow both physically and spiritually and be filled with the love of our Creator."

Jesus put his arms around his mother, held her close, and said: "And each day I thank the Father for you, who gave me life upon this earth. Like the seed that grows in the field, I too will bring life and gifts to many."

Mary Remembers

Mary held the memory of Jesus in her arms as she did when he was first born. As a mother she needed to do this, because her son was dead now, and she could hold him no other way. She tried to drown from her memory the cries of the crowd that had screamed for his crucifixion, with the remembered cries of a hungry child waiting to be fed. But she wasn't very successful.

The cries that she had released as she gave birth to her son seemed lost somewhere among the cries spoken out as she stood beneath his cross, not ready to give him back yet, certainly not in this manner. In birth he had been covered with her blood, in death with his own. In both birth and death her tears had washed blood from his body. Who could ever imagine, she thought, that love would lead him to a cross, that love would be nailed to a cross?

Today was his birthday, and she wondered if she would live to see his next, and if anyone would remember him by then. Love had caused her son's death, and love would soon cause hers, she believed, for she could feel her heart breaking, so much did she want to be with him again.

God's Angels

Send Us a Savior

Two angels cried out to the heavenly Father: "How long will humanity suffer? Listen to the people crying out: 'Let it end. Take us into your loving arms. End this destruction and send us a savior.' But close your ears to those who curse and mock you, oh heavenly Father."

He looked at the two angels and said: "It is my children of whom you speak. They are a part of me, and I am a part of them. I tell you this: When the appointed time has been reached, the battle will begin. The world will be divided. Human beings will divide it with their free will. Those who have been faithful to my rules will come to me, and those who have given their allegiance to the god of darkness must stay with him, for there will be no room for them in my home."

Angels at Jesus' Birth

An angel said: "I do not understand. Why does she cry so hard so soon after her son's birth? Her tears seem to be composed of sorrow rather than of joy." He stared at Mary, whose tears continued to fall upon Jesus as she held him lovingly in her arms.

An older and wiser angel said: "Shush. Be silent and watch. Perhaps she can already see within the gentle marks rubbed on his face during his birth the cruel and savage marks that will cover his body in death."

Just then, Joseph reached over and touched his son's hand, looked proudly into his eyes, and said: "I accept you and love you as my son, and you shall bear my name."

With tears still streaming from her eyes, Mary said as gently as she could: "No, Joseph, he shall be named Jesus."

Sadness struck quickly and painfully at Joseph's heart, but with a firm and strong voice he said: "So be it. His name shall be Jesus." But he didn't raise his eyes from Jesus, fearing Mary might see the disappointment that filled them.

The smaller angel said to the larger one: "Is the child's mother giving him the correct name? After all, it is Joseph who will raise him and provide for him."

The older and wiser angel responded: "It is the right name—the one he should be given. It shall be spoken many times upon the earth in both good times and bad. I tell you this: When he begins to speak, people will remember his words. And the tears his mother sheds now are nothing compared to those that will fall from her eyes when he dies."

Then he began to sing, and one by one other angels joined him until a great chorus had formed, filling every corridor in the heavens with beautiful music. Its warmth reached the earth and filled Mary's heart, easing her sadness and pain, and she began to hum softly to her son. The clouds opened above the stable, and the stars seemed to sparkle and glow at the same time, bringing light into a world filled with so much darkness—the darkness of humankind's failure to care about one another or about God.

A beautiful and powerful angel who had watched from afar, but who had said nothing, appeared suddenly at the side of the two angels and said: "The heavens cast their light upon him now, but he truly is the light of the world—a light that man will take long to fully understand. Spiritual darkness disperses at his sight and even at the mention of his name."

If we look long enough, that light can be found not only in Mary's eyes but in the eyes of every woman, whether she has borne children or not. I believe that God has created women with a special blessing, knowing that one would someday bring his son into the world.

The Shepherd Boy's Amazement

The shepherd boys gathered together because their sheep were about to be sold. There would be nothing for them to do except reminisce and tell the story begun so long ago and handed down from one person to another.

It was a long and lonely night as a shepherd boy sat watching his sheep. He looked up at the sky, and the stars seemed to wink, twinkle, and turn. They were so tiny in the vast darkened sky. But then, as if from a burst of sunlight, a large star appeared—a very bright and shining star.

The young shepherd boy stood up. He was amazed. What was happening? Was a star going to hit the earth? And yet, a part of him knew it was his duty to stay with his sheep. He was a shepherd, after all. And so he sat down and began to think very deeply.

All at once a light appeared. He looked at it. It certainly was a strange light. Then he realized it was an angel. The angel said: "Fear not, I am an angel. I have come here to see you. Do not be frightened. Care for your sheep. But I ask you this; may I have the smallest one? This one?" And the angel gently bent down, picked up a small lamb, and said, "I would like it as a gift."

The shepherd boy shook his head and said, "I cannot give you this lamb. The sheep are not mine. I only care for them."

The angel said, "I will return it to you."

The shepherd boy looked again, thought deeply, and said, "Fine, but it must be returned before the night is up."

Before the night had ended, the angel appeared again, handed the young boy the lamb, and said to him: "It has kept the child warm. It and the child are filled with love." Then a tear fell from the angel's eye and a beautiful sunrise began, truly a gift from the angels on high.

Angels Surround Us

*J*esus sat down on the warm sand and admired the power and beauty of the waves, which seemed to touch the sky. There was no expression on his face, just peace. Peter came to him and said: "Master, Master, come. Aren't you lonely? You have been sitting there for hours. The sun is beating down upon you, and there is much work to be done tomorrow."

Jesus smiled at his friend and answered, "But Peter, I am not alone."

Peter looked around quickly but saw no one. He said, "Master, you have been in the sun too long. Come." And he tried to pull Jesus up.

Jesus replied, "Come, sit down with me."

Peter said: "Master, you do not understand. I have so much work to do."

Jesus gently patted his hand and said: "Peter, Peter, there is time. Be patient, be patient."

Peter sighed and thought, *There he goes again.*

Jesus smiled because he knew what Peter was thinking and asked, "Peter, do you think I am wise?"

Peter answered, "Well, yes, of course you are or I would not be following you. I would not be spending my whole time, my whole life . . . "

Jesus looked at him and Peter immediately became silent. But then Peter said, "I have much to learn. I know this. I am old, Master, but I try."

Jesus responded, "Yes, I know."

Peter said, "When I came here, I saw no one with you, but you said you were not alone."

Jesus put his head close to Peter's ear and said, "There are angels among us."

"Angels?" Peter said and quickly jumped up and looked around. "I don't see anyone." He started waving his hands.

Jesus asked, "Do you have to see them, Peter? Do you not believe what I have told you?"

Peter sat down in a huff and said, "I know what is written, but I have never seen an angel, and so I am not sure if I truly believe in them. What is an angel? What does an angel do for us? Why is it with us?"

Jesus answered: "Many questions, Peter, you ask many questions. The angels are with each and every soul. They are within our heart, mind, and very being. They are there to help guide us, but we must open our heart and mind to them. We must spend time in prayer and doing good works. When we do this, we open the door so that our angel of light may enter and help to guide us. Do you think our Creator, the heavenly Father, would place us upon the earth without a guide?"

Peter thought for a moment and answered, "If this is true, then why can't we see angels?"

Jesus smiled and said: "Maybe because the Father has given us free will and because humans have chosen to sin, we can no longer see such goodness. Yes, we can see the beauty and power in nature, but we cannot see a spirit of light and love. We can see a tree, the sun, the moon, a raindrop, the ocean, and a child. We can feel, but some things we cannot see."

Peter thought for a long time before he said, "Master, will this angel created by the Father stay with us forever, even if we have sinned?"

Jesus answered: "An angel is with every man, woman, and child, and shall be until our final breath. An angel is the Father's kiss of love upon every soul as he breathes life into it."

Jesus Sees Angels

The air was chilling to the bone. The disciples lay huddled together close to a small fire that burned and flickered in the night. The sky was dark except for a few stars that peeked through here and there. Jesus sat staring at the sky, lost in thought. His head was covered with a shawl to keep him warm. Beneath it his eyes seemed to shine and sparkle from the light of the fire as it cast strange shadows over the men. Some were fast asleep, others were dozing, and two were still awake.

Peter broke the silence and asked: "Master, why do you stare at the sky like that? What do you see? What does it tell you?"

Without looking at his friend, Jesus answered: "I see angels. They are spirits who light the night for the traveler and who give comfort to God's children on earth. They tell a story of life and death—a story that none of us fully understands yet."

When the shawl slipped off of Jesus' head, John said, "Master, you must cover your head or you will become cold."

Jesus looked at John and said: "Thank you for your concern, my friend. You are right. The cloth helps to keep the warmth within the body. Have you ever wondered why the Father created the stars?"

They shook their heads, not knowing the answer.

Two other disciples awoke in time to hear his question, and one said: "That's a foolish question. They're just there in the sky. That's all." The other nodded in agreement.

Jesus overhead him and said: "That is not true, my friend. For in the darkness there is light, in the light there is truth, and there is much knowledge to be learned from truth. It is written and it is said that the Father is the one who gives us truth, and truth gives us light so that we have no fear. We have only to follow the brightness of his heart reflected in the stars."

The Father Never Abandons Us

John had great love in his heart for Jesus, who knew so much about life and cared so much about people. Jesus looked up at John and asked, "What do you see, John?"

John smiled and with some embarrassment lowered his eyes to the ground. Then slowly he lifted them until he was looking at Jesus again, and said, "I see a man who I know truly cares."

Jesus smiled back at John and said: "I tell you this, John: The Father has been good to all of us for we do not have to go through life alone, a part of us is always with the Father."

John looked at Jesus with a question in his eyes. This was not the first time that he didn't understand Jesus' words. He said, "Master, I don't understand."

Again Jesus answered: "John, a part of us is always with the Father. The Father never abandons us. But we must open the door to our heart and mind so that we may understand and feel his presence in his love."

"I also believe, John, that he has given us not really another person but a spirit of love who walks with us and teaches us right from wrong when we have opened our heart and mind. Some people believe that our conscience speaks to us, but I think it is an angel whom our Father gives to each soul as life is formed in the womb of the mother. That angel carries that soul at the moment of death to the Father and stands nearby as we are judged."

John blinked. Were his eyes playing tricks on him or was it the sun? Was that a shadow next to Christ? He continued blinking his eyes, but it didn't go away. Jesus smiled his gentle, kind, caring smile, extended his arms, and said: "John, John, you will never be alone. A spirit of love will always be with you."

Jesus Speaks with an Angel

Jesus was enjoying one of those rare moments when he was all alone. He had taught on this spot many times, but it seemed as if he were seeing it for the first time—the rocks, the trees, the earth, the sky. "Everyone should have some time alone like this," he said to himself, surveying the beauty and power of the universe and becoming one with the Father as he did so.

He was tired, so he sat down and leaned against an olive tree, enjoying the warmth of the setting sun upon his face. He couldn't keep his eyes open, and sleep easily overcame him. His rhythmic breathing seemed to match the softly blowing winds. Deep in sleep he saw a bright light, an angel, and many people. Some looked angry, some looked like they were crying, and some had no expression on their faces. But Jesus couldn't hear them, and so he called out to the angel, "I wish to know what they are saying."

The angel whispered with the softest and most beautiful sound of love: "You cannot hear them, for they do not call out to you yet. They speak to the Father."

"But I am his son, am I not?" Jesus said in his dream.

"Yes," said the, angel, "but you still have not shed your . . . " and suddenly the angel was silent.

Jesus woke up to find Peter and John sitting beside him. "Master," Peter said with a large grin, "You sure were tired. You didn't even hear us walk up to you."

Jesus noticed that darkness now filled the sky. "I must have been sleeping for a while," he said.

"Yes, Master," Peter said, "but as you tell us, you wouldn't have slept so long if you didn't need it." Peter grinned again and Jesus smiled his gentle smile.

"My friend, my friend," Jesus said to Peter, "you are a father and still a son." Peter looked confused, but before he could ask him what he meant, Jesus described his dream. When he finished, Jesus said, "Dreams many times tell us what we refuse to see in life."

"Yes," Peter said, "when I was a child, I dreamed often of falling from great heights."

Jesus nodded as if he knew and said, "You had a fear in your life, did you not, Peter?"

"Yes," Peter said, "but I didn't realize it and overcome it until I grew older."

Jesus said, "Dreams are like windows through which we can see life in new ways."

"Should we follow our dreams?" Peter asked.

"Not always," Jesus answered. "But if we understand their true meaning, we can understand our life better."

Mary Feels Weary

Mary stood by the fire. She had tears in her eyes. Her voice trembled as she cried out, "Why?" She was feeling lonely and tired. Her son was now a man—a man who was loved, respected, and sought after by many people. But Mary knew in her heart that she had reason to worry, because she had heard the mumbling, the undertone, and the anger among many people. And yet, she also heard them sing his praise.

She looked at the fire, which was beginning to die. The sparks were no longer strong. But she did not want to waste another stick. She said: "My heart is filled with coldness. I am so frightened and feel so alone."

Then a figure appeared in the doorway. Mary did not recognize the man who stood there and so she asked, "Who are you?"

He answered, "Fear not, Mary, because we have spoken before. I have come from afar. Fear not, for he is the chosen one, and you have been his caretaker. You have taught him well. Fear not, Mary, fear not."

Then, as Mary looked up into the angelical face of the man, he said, "The tears you shed will be many, but remember, there will be many who will speak his name long after the tears have dried."

Harm a Child, and You Harm the Father

*J*esus tried to comfort the woman, whose eyes were red and swollen from crying. "Master," she said, "I left my child here while I went to the well for water, and I don't know where he's gone. I stayed longer than I should have, Master, but never did I believe anyone would take him." She began to cry again, and her tears fell upon Christ's hands.

Jesus was filled with so much sorrow that he thought his heart would break. He lifted up the woman's chin so that he could look into her eyes and said, "Woman, woman, weep not, for the child was a gift."

"Yes, but my gift, Master," she said.

"Yes, I agree," Jesus said. "The child belongs to you, to your husband, and to the Father."

"He is only four, Master, only four and so innocent. Why would anyone take him? I curse them for I fear they intend to harm him. Why would anyone take him?"

Jesus sighed and said, "Woman, woman, there are many in this world who have no heart."

She looked at him rather strangely and asked, "You mean they're not made like us, Master?"

"What I'm saying," Jesus explained, "is that there is no love in their hearts and no respect for the gifts my Father has given to others. I tell you this: I would not want to be included among such people when they enter the gate of my Father's home. To harm a child is to take a knife and cut the heart of my Father."

An old man who stood nearby staring at them said, "Master, doesn't the Father welcome all of those who come to his door in death?"

Jesus said: "I tell you as I have told her. When you harm a child, you harm the Father." Then he looked down at his hands, still damp from the woman's tears, and said: "Woman, woman, ask the Father that the child be returned to your home unharmed and not to his home. But I tell you this: If he is killed, the angels will carry his soul with song to the heavens and the gates of my Father's home shall be opened to him. But those who have harmed him shall suffer a fate worse than death. They shall see their act over and over again, and there will be no peace in their hearts or in their eyes. Their ears shall hear the screams of pain and sorrow that they have inflicted. And when the angel of death comes for them, they shall see the face of that person whose tender and precious life they have destroyed."

What Happens at Your Last Breath?

*J*esus sat in a field of wildflowers whose seeds had been strewn by the winds and the birds. It was truly a beautiful scene—a gift of God untouched by people. He prayerfully thanked the Father for being able to see, touch, and experience such beauty. Those who had come to listen to him were also deeply touched by this scene. They wanted to capture and preserve this moment so that they could continue to enjoy it.

A young but wise man among them said: "Master, when I sit here with you, I see beauty, but when I go into the town, I see suffering. I ask you this: When we breathe our last breath, what happens?"

Jesus looked at the young man and answered: "What do you think happens?"

The crowd began to snicker and laugh. Jesus quickly raised his hand, shook his head and said: "I did not ask this question to make fun of him. Is it not a proper question?" The smiles disappeared and were replaced with looks of concern.

The young man said, "There are so many different beliefs about death, but I feel in my heart that life ends with a person's last breath."

Jesus did not respond. Instead, he reached down and pulled a flower from the earth, snapped off its head, crushed its beauty, and let the petals fall from his hand. He looked down at the earth and remained silent. Then he carefully picked another flower, this time snapping its stem but leaving the root intact. He placed the flower next to his cheek, touched it to his lips, and then he held it high for all to see and said: "At the last moment of life, the Father gives a beautiful gift to us. He gives a special friend to every man, woman, and child. This friend helps us to make the journey from this life to the next. It is someone who has gone before us. The angel of death and the guardian angel who has been with us since the moment of conception and throughout life accompany the person. These three help to make this time of transition a joyful experience. It is like closing a door to one life and opening it to another life. The body remains upon the earth, but the soul—the Father's gift that makes a body human—must return home again. Think of the body as a shell in which the soul is encased. It truly is a gift beyond gifts."

The people looked at one another, and a very old wise man asked, "Master, do we choose who will come for us?"

"No," Jesus answered. "This too is a gift."

"Will I speak to the person who comes for me?"

Jesus said: "When the body and soul divide, it will feel as though a great weight has been lifted off you. You will feel free and experience joy as never before. You have told me that when you look at these flowers and the beautiful and peaceful scene they create, you receive comfort and feel good, but my friends, I tell you this: What you will experience at death is truly a gift that I cannot compare with any other joy you will feel."

The young man who was wise said, "Master, then I am ready to go."

Jesus smiled and said: "No, not now, my son, not now. It is at the will of my Father, not yours or anyone else's."

The flower Jesus held in his hand began to wilt. He looked at it, placed it to his lips, and said: "There is sadness in death, but remember, we are here to learn—to give of ourselves and to share what we have. I truly feel sorry for those who fail to do this, to work with their hands, hearts, and minds."

Jesus gently placed the wilted flower on the earth and said: "I have not disturbed its roots. Another flower, like the soul, will return. What you sow upon the earth, you give spiritually to the Father. Sow good seeds—good deeds and thoughts—and you will leave good memories behind." A soft breeze began to blow. The flowers began to move to a rhythm all their own and the smell of the sea drifted up the hill. Jesus smiled and said: "Come, my friends. Let us go to the city to teach, to heal, and to comfort."

The Riches in the Mind, Heart, and Soul

*A*n angel, very small in stature, came to the heavenly Father and asked: "Lord, why do you spend so much time watching those who dress in mourning colors and live so simply. They till the earth producing new life and care for the animals as if they were a part of their own family."

"And they love their family, don't they?" the Lord quickly added.

The angel nodded a firm yes and continued watching with the heavenly Father as a man got up before the sun rose and began to care for the animals and the fields as if they were precious gifts.

Throughout the day he treated his family and neighbors with respect and caring—sharing whatever he had with them. And yet those who drove by from that world just outside his world stared and thought how strange these people were. How could anyone live without modern conveniences—no television, no radio, no running water, no gas, no electricity. Certainly God provided all these things for us and wants us to have them. The man was too busy with his own thoughts to hear God saying: "Yes, but at what expense? Of what value is it if you gain the whole world but lose your soul?"

The heavenly Father looked at the small angel and said: "Oh little one, do you see what inner peace they have found? They live close to the earth, but they live on my love. Many who live in varying degrees of greater comfort and convenience speak my name, often in beautiful churches, but to whom and to what have they given their hearts? How often do they think of me each day, and what do they do just for me each day? Others may condemn those who do not follow the ways of the world in order to draw closer to me, but I will not. I have chosen some to live in the simplest of ways so that others in seeing them may be blessed by being reminded that the only important riches are those that can be stored in the heart, the mind, and the soul."

Restore Peace

*J*esus knelt on the ground, his head resting on a large rock. There were tears in his eyes as he slowly raised his head and cried out:

"Father, Father, let there be peace. Give peace to the world, and give peace to me."

An angel whispered very softly into his ear, "Humankind must restore the peace which its sins have destroyed."

A beam of light from the heavens suddenly fell on Jesus' head. He looked in the direction from which it was coming and said: "Father, Father, have you heard my prayer? Is this a sign that there will be peace on the earth and in my heart?"

The angel whispered again into his ear: "Peace, peace, peace. It should blow freely like the winds throughout the earth, forever moving like the waters. But it is heavy and still, Master, like the rock upon which your tears fall. On the earth, peace is a heavy burden, and it takes much effort to restore it."

Jesus Weeps for Joseph

Jesus longed to be held once again by his father's rough but gentle hands. Joseph had always been a quiet man and yet a man of great strength. Jesus knew that he would not see his father again before he died. He remembered looking at his father's hands, and now he looked at his own. They weren't as rough and calloused as they used to be. He whispered: "I was content then, and yet I longed for something I didn't understand. Now I long for the contentment that I once had."

His tears released memories from his heart, and he remembered a story his father had told him about when he, Joseph, was but a child. His father and his uncle were making a long trip to visit a friend when they came upon a horrible scene filled with suffering, pain, and death. Four lepers lay by the side of the road, bleeding to death, and crying out, "Help us, help us." One called out in a horrible whisper for water.

Jesus remembered how Joseph had told him: "I wanted to run from the sight, but my brother held me back. He said, 'Look at them but don't touch them.' It was a scene I never forgot." Jesus recalled with pride that Joseph had overcome the initial fear of not knowing what to do and had run to get some water, realizing nothing more could be done for them. Jesus also remembered what Joseph told him when he asked him why men were so cruel, especially to those who were already suffering so much. His words were: "My son, it seems as though it has always been that way and always will be. But I tell you this: We can help to alleviate it."

Then Jesus' mind switched to another scene when he, as a young boy, and his mother came across a prostitute who had been beaten very badly. Mary drew water from a well and gave her a drink. He remembered asking Mary a question similar to the one he had asked his father: "Mother, why did people do this to her? Is it because of what she did? Did she steal someone's coins?"

Mary answered: "People hurt one another thoughtlessly. Maybe they try to take out the pain of their sins on others."

Jesus continued to look at his hands and recalled many similar incidents, and then he looked up into the sky and said, "Why, Father?" His tears began to dry, or would it be more proper to say they were beginning to heal? His hands had changed from the way they were when he worked alongside his father. Now his life was changing, and it was alongside his Father in heaven that he must work. But still he cried out once more: "Why, Father, why?" He remembered the tears in Joseph's eyes when he told Jesus his story, and the sorrow and compassion in his mother's eyes while she wiped the bloody face of the badly beaten prostitute.

And then it came to him, and he wondered why he had not realized it before: For all the evil that is to be found in one person's heart, mind, or hands, God always fills someone else's heart with compassion to transform it. Jesus looked at his hands again. Often he was drawn to them without knowing why. A beam of light seemed to fall upon them as he folded them in prayer.

And an angel wept as she whispered in his ear: "Master, your hands shall carry the sins of all humanity and be nailed to a cross, but they shall take death and transform it to life." And one by one, all of the angels in heaven wept—in sorrow for his pain, but in joy because he would soon be coming home again, and the gates of heaven would again be opened upon his arrival.

Angels at Jesus' Death

As Jesus hung on the cross, he heard a strange sound—no louder than the whisper of a gentle breeze making its way through a tree. Could it be his Father? Although he didn't see him and couldn't understand why his Father would allow him to suffer so much, he knew he was there. As he tried to turn his head toward the sound, the nails pulled at his torn flesh and pain shot through his entire body. No one was there. But as he turned back and looked down at Mary, his mother, and at John and Mary Magdalene, the pain in his heart and mind was even worse. It hurt more than his body. He cried out in his heart: "Father, the pain has become unbearable. Take it away from me. For I did not mock you in the temple, in the streets, or in the fields. I only told people to give you the love due to you. But still, Father, I accept the pain."

Silence filled his ears. No longer could he hear the laughter, shouts, or jeers of the soldiers or the crowd. An angel sang to him the sweetest and gentlest of songs, "Master, Master, Master, you are the Son of God."

Jesus thought the pain must be playing tricks on his mind. But the angel sang the same song to him again, and Jesus called out, "Who speaks to me?"

A soldier called out in mockery, "Maybe it's your Father coming to take you down from the cross."

Jesus looked up into the sky and wondered how much longer he could suffer this great pain that thumped and throbbed and beat at his body. Again he heard the gentle song of an angel as she touched his crown of thorns, "My Master, fear not, for each drop of blood you shed is a precious gift for all humankind."

Jesus hung limp on the cross, and no more tears came from his eyes to wash the blood away, for his body had been drained of every drop of moisture.

Angels began to sing all around him now. Different tunes and different words from each, but they all blended together beautifully. One was singing: "Come, my lord, and give me your soul. Let me hold and comfort you. Let me hold and comfort you."

Another angel sang a song no one heard, except perhaps Mary: "Weep no more, my children. Weep no more, my children. He has died upon a cross of pain and suffering. But now his love will come to all. Now his love will come to all."

An angel whispered in Mary's ear, "He has returned to his Father's home."

Mary, like her son, had no tears left. Mother Nature joined in the angel's song, and the earth began to rumble.

One man cried out, "Master, save us." But his voice was lost like a whisper in a mighty storm. His Master had died.

Jesus Teaches His Apostles

Similar Words

Jesus was awakened by Peter, Andrew, and John, who were shouting, "Master! Master! Master!" He wiped his sleepy eyes, raised his hand in acknowledgment, and got up and went down to the water to wash his face. Peter was walking a short distance behind the others. His staff dug deep into the earth because his full weight was upon it. His leg was very sore, he was tired and angry, his face was as red as the setting sun, and so he sat down on a rock. The other two disciples ran up to Jesus.

"What is bothering you?" Jesus asked. "I have never seen the three of you like this before."

"That's because you don't know what we heard," John responded.

Peter nodded in agreement, and Andrew said, "Master, I have never been as angry as I was in the city today."

Jesus looked at Andrew and said: "Well then, tell me about it."

Andrew said: "Master, a man was preaching at the home of our friend, the merchant. Can you believe that he would allow anyone to come into his house to speak about the Father?"

Jesus did not respond.

Andrew continued: "This man, I have seen him before. I know I have seen him somewhere. Isn't that right, Peter?"

Peter hunched his shoulders and said: "I am certain . . . "

But before he could finish, Jesus said: "But you are not. Be honest now and do not lie to me."

Andrew replied: "But Master, he spoke almost the same words as you do when you tell about the Father. Can you imagine that? He has no claim to the Father."

Jesus shook his head and said: "Andrew, we are all children of the Father."

"Yes, I know that," Andrew answered, "but Master . . . "

"Does he claim to be the Son of God?" Jesus asked.

Peter responded: "No, I cannot say that, but he may have. How are we to know? When we came upon him, he was speaking your words."

Jesus broke out into a beautiful smile. The men were shocked. "You are not angry?" Peter asked.

"Of course not," Jesus answered, "for now I know my words are being spread throughout the town."

"But you are not the one speaking them," Peter replied.

"Is it so important," Jesus asked, "that I speak them, for they came from my heart and from my lips?"

"But maybe they weren't exactly the same words," John objected.

"Is that so terrible?" Jesus asked.

John shook his head and said, "You mean we hurried from the city without even stopping to rest or to eat and drink, and you are not concerned or upset?" In frustration and anger he knocked over Peter's staff, which had been leaning against a rock. Jesus said, "It is better to take out your anger on nature than on a person."

John was deeply embarrassed as Peter bent down and picked up the staff he used to support himself.

Jesus said: "My friends, be understanding toward others because that is the will of my father. He does not want people to quarrel over my words but to understand and express them, each in his or her own way. No harm is done as long as the truth remains." And then he looked out over the water and said: "I washed my face with these waters. If another man comes along and washes his face with them, is that wrong?

"If I look at the sun and feel its warmth, is it wrong for others to do the same? Remember, we are all the father's children. The words I have spoken are the Father's, but you must not forget that others have also been inspired. I am inspiring you so that you too will preach the words of the father. Be patient and let peace reign in your hearts. For many will claim to have known, to have seen, and to have been with my Father, but you will know the truth."

Jesus looked at Peter's staff and said: "Your staff has both helped and hindered you because you have become dependent on it. And as much as I would like to, I cannot heal you. Not everyone can be healed, and not all can understand the words of my Father. We each have our own duties to carry out in this life."

The disciples looked at one another and a calm like the gentle ripples of the waves came over them. Each in his own way thought: He truly is the Master. His gentleness and caring are above reproach.

They all were inspired. Their tongues were loosened and knowledge began to grow like the seeds in the fields to fill their minds.

Teachers of the Word

Jesus and his friends sat around the fire. They felt warm and comfortable. There was no sign of the rain that Jesus knew would come in the morning. Peter, like the others, had eaten well, and now it was time to talk about what had happened that day. He said, "Master, are we not good students and followers of yours?"

Jesus was surprised by his question and answered, "Yes, my friend, but surely you already know this."

"But, Master," Peter asked, "who will carry the message after we are all gone?"

Jesus shook his head and said: "My friend, my friend, many men and women listen to us and then tell others what they have heard."

"But they don't tell them everything," John remarked.

"That is true," Jesus said, "but each one has something different to tell. Our words shall spread all over the world the Father has created."

The men sat there with wonder in their eyes. "How can this be?" they asked one another.

Jesus smiled and said, "Look up. What do you see?"

"Darkness," one answered.

"Stars," another said.

And a third replied, "The moon."

Jesus said, "Other people throughout this world are watching the same sky that you now see." He scooped up a handful of dirt, a stone, and a twig. He held his hand high so that they could all clearly see it in the light from the fire. Slowly the earth fell between his fingers, and then the stone, and finally the twig. He immediately scooped them up again and repeated the same procedure a second, a third, and a fourth time.

They looked at one another as a large tear rolled down his cheek. There was silence. Only the cracking of the fire could be heard. He breathed a deep sigh and said: "People's minds are like this earth, this stone, and this twig. It is in the earth that a seed grows. Stones are used to build a house. Twigs are burned to start a fire and cook food." They still did not understand him, so Jesus said: "All three are necessary if the words of my Father are to remain firmly rooted in the hearts, minds, and souls of faithful people where they will be remembered, thought about, shared with others, and explained. Words need an open heart and mind where they can grow. Words need a home where their true meaning will be protected. Words reveal truths that give life."

Feeding on God's Words

When Peter noticed Jesus spreading seeds in a field they were passing, he asked him: "Master, why are you doing that? Who will harvest them when they grow?"

"The hungry," Jesus answered.

"But how will they find it?" Peter wanted to know.

Jesus looked at Peter and said, "When one hungers, one can find food—whether it is for the body, the heart, or the mind." Jesus sat down and asked, "You think I'm foolish, don't you, Peter?"

"Well, yes, Master. You don't even know who owns this ground."

Jesus shook his head and said with a smile: "Peter, my friend, I do know. Everything belongs to my Father. I sow seeds that give life. You and the others will sow seeds of truth to guide others when I am gone."

Peter asked, "Master, what are you trying to tell me?"

"I am telling you, Peter, that when I am gone, my Father's words will still live."

"Oh, Master, do not speak of death."

"Do not be foolish, Peter. Death comes to all."

"But you are the Son of God."

Jesus smiled again and said, "Peter, I am like you, born of woman." He looked over to where he had scattered the seeds. "Those who are hungry will come and eat, and hopefully they will save a few of the seeds to plant and begin new life. No one lives by bread alone, or only by my Father's words. Both together give life."

"But Master," Peter asked, "who will speak your Father's words when you're gone?"

"You will do with my words what I have done with the seeds, Peter. You will plant them in the hearts of many, and a few of those who come after you—inspired by those truths deeply rooted within them—will do the same and inspire still others. My Father's light shall fill them with wisdom and understanding, and when they speak, people will listen."

Peter stood silently, thinking for a long time, and then asked: "Master, will everyone follow your Father's rules in the same way?"

Once again Jesus smiled and answered: "No, Peter. People will interpret my Father's words in different ways. Does not the wind blow in different directions, and does not the rain fall in different places? My Father's words will be written in many languages so that the wise may study them, discover new meaning within them, and more clearly understand my Father's will and his ways. But I tell you this, Peter: The commandments given to Moses will never change. They must stand like stone until the end of time. And my Father's love for his creatures shall never dim."

Peter seemed content and picked a seed off a rock. "Do not destroy it, Peter. If it has fallen, it is the will of my Father. Perhaps the rain will wash it into fertile soil where it can root and grow."

"Then it is the Father who gives life to all?" Peter asked.

"My Father has made the seed and given it to us, but we must find fertile ground in which to place it."

Roundabout Stories

*J*esus boarded the boat with John, and they rowed out a good distance from the shore where they relaxed for a while, enjoying the calm waters and the blue skies, the peace and the quiet. "Isn't it beautiful out here, Master?"

Jesus didn't answer. He seemed to be lost in thought, in prayer. John became a little annoyed and impatient when Jesus didn't respond, and so he said in a voice loud enough to attract his attention, "Master, you've got to get away from people once in a while."

Jesus said firmly: "No, John. For however long my Father gives me, I shall walk the earth and speak his words to as many as will listen to them."

Jesus had responded to John's impatience with kindness and truth, and so John, feeling very foolish all of a sudden, decided it might be best to change the subject of their conversation and asked, "Master, why do you teach us some things in such roundabout ways, with stories and parables?"

A gentle but brilliant smile filled Jesus' face, for he recognized what John was doing, but he also knew his question was asked sincerely and honestly. "John, John," he said, "you have been with me for such a long time, and still you don't understand? Like the petals that make up a flower, my stories have many levels of meaning. But when the petals are removed one by one, you can gradually see into the heart and soul of one of my Father's truths."

"But, Master," John said, "I still don't understand, for you have answered my question with still another image."

"And neither do I always understand," Jesus said. "I tell you only what my Father tells me. No one fully understands my Father's wisdom." Jesus leaned over the edge of the boat and looked at the image of his face reflected in the water. He poked it with his finger, causing ripples, and said, "And many will distort my Father's words, twisting and turning them to suit their own needs or using them to condemn and attack others. Sticks can be used to beat an animal or another human being, or they can be gathered to give warmth and bake bread. Words too can be used in many ways. My Father forms his rules with them, and not too long ago, John, you used words to express your impatience. Words, like the leaves on a tree, were created to give comfort and shelter. Stories help people to remember my Father's words, and in remembering them, to think about them, to discover their meaning, and to apply it to their own lives. There are still many truths to be learned about the earth, the sea, and the sky, and there are still many truths to be learned about my Father's words."

Faithful to God's Word

The disciples returned to be with Jesus. It was a quiet gathering because there were only four of them—Peter, Andrew, John, and Jesus. The others were off on tasks Jesus had given to them, but Jesus was pleased to spend the evening with these three. As they silently ate together, John stoked the fire to keep them warm against the chill of the night.

Then John said, "Master, it is good to be back with you. This opportunity is a gift because there are so few of us, and this is a pleasant, calm, and peaceful night. I hope you will give us lots of time to ask you questions."

Jesus nodded and replied, "Have I not always encouraged you to ask questions?"

John replied, "Yes, but what I want to discuss with you is personal."

Peter and Andrew were surprised at John's remarks, and Peter said, "And we are not permitted to listen?"

John smiled apologetically and answered, "No. I enjoy being with you, but this is something I have held deep in my heart since the first time I heard the Master's words."

John thought for a moment and then asked, "Master, what must one do to be your disciple, to follow you and your teachings faithfully?"

Jesus smiled gently and said, "John, you have been with me for some time. You have listened to me teach, you have eaten with me, and we have all slept together near the fire at night to keep warm. In fact, you are the one who stokes the fire to keep it going. The flames are like the words I speak, but you and many others after you will stoke the fire in my words to bring warmth and comfort to many people. My Father's words are like the sea. They will flow forever. Like the rain that cleanses the earth, people's sins will be washed away. The clouds in the sky are like angels whispering to us and telling us that there is a better life, a life of peace and understanding.

"It is not easy for anyone to live according to my words. My path may seem strange or mysterious, but it is a path to spiritual growth and inner peace along which many will walk in response to the words of my Father. But I tell you, in fact I warn you, that this path is not easy, even though it is filled with great love, inner peace, and harmony.

"Do unto others what you would want them to do to you. Give them comfort and understanding. Do not treat a servant badly. Do not take a woman just to bear your children. Do not take words from the scriptures without fully understanding them."

Then Jesus took John's hand, they stoked the fire together, and Jesus said: "If people work in harmony with the Creator, there will be peace.

But if they refuse, destruction will spread throughout the earth like an uncontrolled forest fire."

John said: "You speak many different words. Some are comforting and others are frightening."

Jesus said, "Yes, the world is that way because of sin."

Words Reveal Truth

The men sat listening to every word of a storyteller. Jesus along with Judas and Peter walked slowly toward the group and saw how the men seemed to be mesmerized by the words the storyteller spoke. Judas said to Peter: "I cannot understand why these people are so interested in stories. They are nothing but lies."

Jesus touched Judas's hand and said, "My friend, listen and you will learn something." And so, the three of them stood and listened to the man tell one story after another. When he was finished, a basket was passed among those present and coins were placed in it.

Jesus went up to the man and said, "My friend."

The man looked at Jesus and said, "You are no friend of mine, but I know who you are. You also tell stories, as I do, but I am told you do not pass the basket afterward."

Jesus laughed. "My friend, my friend, it is not necessary for me to pass the basket. If people wish to give us coins to buy the bread we eat or to give to the poor, we thank them. But even when no one gives us coins, we are always provided for in some other way. There are very few nights when we have been hungry."

The man looked deep into Jesus' eyes and said, "Stories reveal life's truths to us. Is this not true?"

Jesus nodded and said: "What you say is true. Stories are a gift to us. We learn from them, and what we learn is remembered, perhaps years later."

Jesus continued, "I, too, tell truths to inspire and guide people. To the crowds who hear them, they seem to be simply stories." Then he looked down at his sandals, bent down, and brushed the sand and dust from his feet, and said: "Life is filled with many mysteries. We all walk along different paths at different times in different ways, but we all eventually come to the same gate."

Then he looked up at the storyteller and said, "We are each born to die, but we leave to those who must continue to walk the path of life after us words that will inspire them."

Words Spoken with Compassion and Love

*P*eter sat silently, lost in thought. John quietly approached him and said in a whisper, "Peter, Peter, do you hear me?"

Peter looked up with anger in his eyes and answered: "Of course I hear you. My leg may be lame but my hearing is fine. Thank you!"

John smiled and then Peter began to laugh and asked, "What troubles you, John?"

John replied: "You sound like the Master. You speak his very words, but not with his compassion and love. You speak them with . . . well, I do not mean to be cruel, but like a cranky, disgusted, tired, sick, old man."

Peter said, "I do not understand you."

"Neither do I," John replied, and they both laughed.

While they were speaking, Jesus slowly approached them. He asked: "My friends, what great discussion are you engaged in? What problem are you trying to solve?"

They answered, "Nothing, Master, nothing."

"I was just teasing Peter," John explained, rather sheepishly.

Peter said, "They were words, only words, Master. I pay no attention to one like him."

Jesus said, "My friends, do you not understand the importance of words? They are like drops of precious water to thirsty person, like a crust of bread to a hungry child. They can take away pain and inspire. They can give comfort and joy."

Peter looked deeply into Jesus' eyes and said: "Master, when you speak to us, you always remind us that your words are the words of the Father. Have you no words of your own to speak?"

John was surprised by Peter's question and said, "You have asked a good question, Peter, a very good question."

Jesus answered: "The words I speak are the words that will be repeated long after we are gone. The words shall never die. They will be interpreted in different ways, but they will never die. I speak the words of the Father, which have strength in them like the mountains. They refresh like water. They bear fruit like the trees. They will carry humanity through many trying times."

The Distortion of Jesus' Words

Peter spoke to Jesus. "Master," he said, "I am very upset."

Jesus replied, "I can see that."

"Master, why do they take your words, twist them, and say they are yours? You speak in such simple terms. I can't always understand others, but I can understand you, Master."

Jesus smiled in appreciation, placed his hand on Peter's shoulder, and said: "Peter, Peter, my friend, many in the world will hear my words but not understand their true meaning. They will interpret them in their own way. But fear not, for there will always be someone to clarify them.

"If a weaver begins a tapestry and is not careful in counting the stitches, it will not hang straight when it is finished. And even though it was woven with great love and caring, it will not hang properly. One can look at it with the eye and discover that errors were made at the beginning."

Then Jesus looked down at the earth, bent down, scooped up a handful of dirt, let it trickle from his fingers, and said, "We were created from dust and unto dust we shall return. But my Father's words are very strong. Even though individuals will at times be unjust, righteousness will prevail, as will the words of my Father."

Words as Gifts

Jesus knew that it was going to be a long and difficult day, and he was already tired. He thought back to a time when he was a child and his mother took him with her to hear a man people said was inspired by the Father. She seemed excited and happy, but pensive, as she packed two small loaves of bread and some dried fish. He remembered how his mother had told him that the Father gives gifts of wisdom and knowledge to many people, not only to those in the temple.

Jesus sat lost in these thoughts and memories, almost able to taste the hard bread and salty fish, when Peter and John approached him and John said: "Master, it is time for us to go. What are you going to teach today? . . . Master, did you hear what I said?"

Jesus was a little startled and answered: "My friends, I am sorry. I was lost in thought. I was thinking about a time in my childhood when I went with my mother to visit a man who was inspired by the Father. And now people are coming to see me for the same reason. You asked what I will speak about. I never know until the crowd begins to come. When the people gather around me, it seems as though I am lifted up. The thoughts come, and I begin to speak. I know I am able to touch people's hearts and to enlighten their minds, and I know that we are all being blessed by the Father."

John said, "Master, a good speaker does a lot of preparation."

Peter nodded in agreement, and Jesus said: "In some cases that is true, but the preparation is done for me. It is a gift of the Spirit. I speak and it comes forth."

"But, Master," John asked, "aren't you afraid when they ask you so many questions? After all, you are not a schooled man."

Jesus smiled and said: "Be patient, my friend. The words will come to me, and they will be filled with wisdom. They will inspire many people. They will be carried throughout the world and never forgotten. They will last until the end of time."

Speaking the Truth

*P*eter said to Jesus, "Master, I must speak to you."

Jesus replied, "Then speak, my friend."

Peter sat down. Jesus could see that he was tired and troubled, and he said to him, "What is on your mind?"

"Well, I have to tell you," Peter answered. "You must be careful about what you say."

Jesus started to smile and said: "The words I speak, Peter, are from the Father. They are not my own words. I only speak them."

"Well, one of these days you're going to be stoned because of what you say," Peter warned.

The smile on Jesus' face grew wider, and he said, "They do not stone a person for what he says, only when a woman is caught in adultery."

Peter shook his head in disagreement and said: "Master, there is already a lot of grumbling in the city, and on the hillsides people are saying you do not speak from our scriptures, which were written long ago, but instead are speaking untruths and making false claims."

Jesus suddenly became very serious and said: "Peter, Peter, I only speak what the Father has inspired me to say." And then he looked down at the ground as tears began to form in his eyes. His shoulders drooped. Peter felt sorry for him because he seemed to age before his very eyes. Then Jesus looked up at Peter and said: "Peter, I must speak only the words I know are true. I cannot bend like this twig I hold in my hand. It will snap when it reaches its breaking point. Those who believe they are speaking the truth are given a special light of inspiration from the Father. But if they lie in order to make their own point or to draw attention to themselves"—and with that he snapped the twig—"then they turn their back on the Father and deny him."

Jesus was silent for a while and then said: "What if all people could be like a tree instead of a twig, strong in their conviction? In their love for the Father, giving warmth and understanding to one another, the earth would be a better place."

Powerful Words

*J*esus looked closely at his disciples, although it seemed like he was looking into them, and he listened to what they were discussing. They didn't realize he was there until he said, "How long have you been with me?" One began to count on his fingers, one looked quizzically into the sky, one stared at the fire, one slowly surveyed the ground, and one took a twig and began to make marks in the soil.

Jesus watched while their minds raced to find an answer. After waiting a while, he broke the silence and said: "Again I ask, how long have you been with me?"

Peter said, "Master, we're still trying to figure it out."

"Has it been that long?" Jesus asked?

"No," Peter said, "but when you've been filled with love and knowledge as we have been by you, time has a way of passing very quickly without being measured."

Luke said, "Yes, Master, you have taught me how to heal with the power of your words."

"And you have taught me how to understand people," Simon added.

Each of them recounted what he had received from Jesus.

Judas spoke last, "Master, I have learned much and I have received much, but I have been given the greatest of gifts—the invitation to walk in your footsteps."

Jesus sighed, wishing Judas had spoken these words from his heart, and said, "Judas, Judas, you are clever, but you still have so much to learn." Judas was insulted by the Master's words and turned to leave. "Do not leave, my friend," Jesus said, "for one learns a new gift each day."

"Learns," said Peter, "or earns?"

Jesus smiled and said: "You are wise, Peter, for one both learns and earns on the earth before receiving his reward in my Father's home. Life is difficult upon the earth for no one is ever totally free from sorrow or temptation. I tell you this: If you live according to my words and my Father's rules, you will do no wrong."

Luke said, "But, Master, they are not Caesar's rules."

And Judas added: "If we don't have any money, your Father won't give it to us. We have to work for it."

Jesus said: "My Father gives gifts to all that Caesar can give to none—soil to grow wheat, a mind to learn, a heart to feel, hands to work, and ten simple rules as a guide through life. If people use these gifts well, Caesar will not find fault with them—and neither will my Father."

John said, "Master, I'm still not sure how long we have been with you."

Jesus responded: "I only asked this because I heard your idle talk. There is so much I have to teach you in so little time. When we come together, we should inspire one another, teach one another, and share one another's gifts, working and praying together, asking the Father for the love we need each day, both for ourselves and for others. The more we give to one another, the more we will receive from him when we call out to him. When we share what we have to eat and drink, we give to him. Whoever shares will share also in one of my Father's greatest gifts—a place in his home."

Jesus, Peter, John, and Judas

The Role of Jesus' Disciples

Jesus broke the bread as his disciples sat around a fire. When it was passed to Peter, he held it longer than Judas thought he should. And so Judas asked, "Peter, are you not going to share the bread with the rest of us?"

John said, "Peter seems deep in thought."

"Yes," Peter replied rather angrily, "and you have broken my concentration."

"What were you thinking?" Jesus asked. "I was thinking about my wife," Peter answered. Tears began to flow from his eyes and he said, "The bread reminds me so much of her, of her love for me. She knew how much I love bread and a good meal."

Judas asked, "Then I have not cooked a good meal tonight?"

The men began to laugh because they knew Judas was mocking Peter.

Peter said, "Out of my way," and he got up rather angrily and stalked off.

When he came back, the men had finished eating, and so Jesus handed Peter his portion of the meal and said, "We saved this for you, Peter, because we knew you would be hungry."

"And that your stomach would growl the whole night, and I would not be able to sleep," John added. The men chuckled.

Then Jesus said: "There are many kinds of love. There is the love that a man and woman share; there is love that a child gives to its parents; there is love among friends."

Then Jesus sighed and said: "My love for my mother is always active and never ends. I have seen the love in my father's eye for my mother. She was often tired, but there was always love in her heart for us. I remember when Mark, a crippled boy, would come to see my mother. He always brought her flowers from the hillside. Mother would smile gently and say, 'They are the most beautiful flowers I have ever seen.' They were ordinary, even slightly wilted flowers, but they were given to her with so much love. Mother would give him some bread she had baked, and his eyes would light up. I remember this from my childhood."

Jesus continued: "Love is shared in so many different ways, by listening to, by caring for, by spending time with another. I have watched the women at the well as they talked, and there was a kind of caring among them."

"Yes, a sharing of gossip," Peter interjected, and the men laughed.

"Yes, maybe it is gossip, but it is a type of caring as they share their life with one another. It is not all gossip, Peter."

Then Jesus looked at Peter, who had finished his meal, and asked, "Do you feel better now, Peter?"

Peter answered, "My stomach is full but my heart still longs for my family."

Jesus reached down, patted him on the shoulder, and said: "Peter, you have given up much, and it is understandable that you long for them. But what you will do will not be forgotten. Your path may be through sorrow at times, but when you reach the home of my Father, you will understand how important a role you have been given."

છે

A Lesson from an Olive

*J*esus sat under an olive tree, slowly munching an olive. Peter commented, "Master, you look so content."

"I am," Jesus replied. "It has been a wonderful day. I feel good when I know that those who have come to hear me are pleased and return home with the knowledge they are loved by the Father and are willing to try to make the world better for those yet to be born and those who are here now."

John said, "Master, at times there are many questions in my mind, but today I only want to be with you; I do not even want to ask you anything."

Peter nodded: "I understand you, John, for I too have many questions to ask the Master. But today the beauty I see all around me fills me with contentment. I feel as I do when I am on the water, casting my nets. It is strange but it is almost like I can feel life itself. When I am on a boat and the waters surround me, I feel alone but protected. I feel special, perhaps because the boat is mine, and the waters seem to be mine also."

John began to laugh and said: "That's because there is no one around you. They know you are a terrible fisherman."

Jesus said, "It is good to think about joyful times and even sad and trying times, and to reflect on them, because when we use our mind and recall such moments, much wisdom can be gained." The men looked at one another, not fully understanding his words. Jesus added: "I have taught you now for many days and many nights. When you leave me, you will have much knowledge. You will lose some of it, and then it will flow back into your mind once again like a stream into a river."

Then he looked down, gathered the pits of the olives he had eaten, and said, "These look like stones that will never grow because they are hard and bear no life. But when these pits are planted, they will grow new life. We are a lot like these seeds."

Peter said, "I do not understand, Master."

Jesus replied: "You will, Peter, in time you will." He handed Peter a rock and said, "Build upon this, Peter, and it will bear fruit like this olive pit."

Prejudice

*A*s Jesus stood under an olive tree, John asked: "Master, are you hungry? If you are, I'll pick some olives for you."

"No, thank you," Jesus answered. "I'll get my own."

He reached up and pulled off an unripe olive.

John and Peter looked at him, and Peter asked, "Master, is your eyesight getting bad?"

"No," Jesus answered. "Why do you ask?"

"Well, Master," Peter said, "even though I'm older than you and my eyes are worse than yours, I can see from here that that olive is not ripe. It will have a bitter taste. It will make your mouth pucker, and it will bite at your tongue."

Jesus smiled and said, "Taste it, my friend." Peter began to laugh, believing Jesus was only kidding. "Take it and eat it," Jesus urged Peter again.

Peter realized Jesus was serious, and he said, "Master, do you realize what you're asking me to do?"

Jesus didn't say anything but simply held the olive out to Peter. Peter bit into the unripe olive. He slowly chewed it until he reached the hard stone center. He grimaced. Then Jesus picked an olive that was a little more ripe, gave it to Peter, and said, "Eat this one now." Peter again took a bite and made a sour face. Jesus then picked a ripe olive, a real beauty, and gave it to Peter. "Now eat this one."

Peter was pleased because he was sure this one would remove the bitter, biting taste of the other two from his mouth. He started to bite it but then said, "Master, why did you do this to me?"

Jesus answered: "The prejudice in life can be compared to an unripe olive. Even though an olive is unripe, it is still beautiful, is it not? When one tastes sin for the first time, it seems delicious, but it causes guilt and remorse. Even that soon passes and what seemed bitter at first becomes sweet. But when one tastes goodness, no bitterness or guilt is left in the heart or mind. Nature can teach us much, Peter."

Peter smiled, and John gave him some water to wash away the bitter taste in his mouth. Jesus took a handful of very ripe olives, gave them to Peter with a smile of his own, and said: "Learn well, my friend. Nature often has wisdom for those who observe."

What Makes a Good Teacher?

*I*t had been a long and tiring day, but a good day. Jesus was pleased. There was a gentleness in his voice that touched the hearts of his disciples. Jesus was also glad that there was food for all to eat. As they shared the meal, Peter asked, "Master, what makes you a good teacher?"

Jesus replied, "Peter, are you questioning my ability?"

"Oh no, no, no, no, no, no," Peter answered. The others laughed.

Jesus smiled, held back his own laughter and said, "What makes a good teacher? Well, I will tell you, Peter. Teachers must have a strong foundation. They must know that what they say is true, and they must express themselves in such a way that others will hunger for the knowledge they offer. Teachers must have strong convictions. But they must also be gentle and caring. They must not hide from people and refuse to impart knowledge to others. They must want to share it. They must be willing to inspire others and be willing to accept many hardships in doing so. The life of a teacher is not easy. Stones of hatred, greed, and envy will be thrown in their way. They must know how to teach the truth to the best of their ability. Their words must inspire others and be like a staff to help guide those who come to learn from them."

John said, "Peter, do you think the Master fills these requirements?"

But before Peter could answer, Jesus said: "That is a difficult question. Only you who have listened to me, walked with me, and supped with me will know if I am a good teacher. Remember, we must learn from one another. I have taught you to the best of my ability, and soon each and every one of you will go out and teach others. You must be strong like a tree. Your beliefs must have firm roots. Your knowledge must be full and continue to grow. You must plant many seeds of knowledge in others. Remember, my Father's love is unending."

Peter said, "But I am an old man, Master."

Jesus replied, "Peter, you are like a rock; you are strong and hard, but there is a gentleness and a caring about you."

"Is it wrong to be hard?" John asked.

"No," Jesus answered. "A tree is hard, but it can bend and break. A rock is strong and is used for building. No fire can destroy it. You, Peter, among all those who are here with me, your name shall be remembered as a rock." The disciples looked at one another.

Judas asked, "Master, what about me?"

Jesus smiled gently and said, "Judas, you too will be remembered, but in another way."

Then he looked down at the earth and said: "My friends, I ask that you pray with me for wisdom and strength so that our words may never die. Go, when it is time, and inspire others so that the chain of love will never be broken, so that the seeds of knowledge may continue to bear fruit and give new life to future generations."

Beautiful Memories

*J*esus saw the worried look on Peter's face. "What troubles you, my friend?" he asked.

Tears began to form slowly in Peter's tired eyes. "I have been told that I am going to be a grandfather. My oldest son will once again present us with a child," Peter answered.

"That should make you happy," Jesus said.

"In many ways it does," Peter replied, "but this world is so troubled. Although I feel much joy in my heart, there is also sadness in it. When I brought my children to the temple, I remember my wife saying 'We are giving this child to the Father so that he may guide him and care for him.' I became resentful. For a part of me thought that it was my child and I could raise him the way I wanted. But I was also respectful, for I knew the Father was aware of what was in my heart. I wanted him to be a part of my son's life and to guide him. I have six children, five beautiful sons and a daughter who has been a great comfort. Even now I know that my wife is happy, and I am filled with joy, for I believe I am here for a reason, Master."

"Yes, Peter" Jesus said, "there is a purpose, and yes you have raised a fine family. I remember a story my mother tells of how when she held me and cried, my father said, 'Weep not, Mary, for you have given the world a son.' My mother replied, as she has repeated many times to me, 'But what will happen to this child?'"

There was silence among the men. It seemed as if each of them was thinking about the stories his mother had told him.

Then Jesus smiled and said, "We all have beautiful memories because our parents were good to us and gave us love and life."

John said: "I do not remember my mother or father. I was raised by others. I hungered to know my parents, but I remember only the sad stories told to me about them. I was wanted, and yet I was not."

Jesus held out his arms and said: "But, John, at least you know something about them. And look what you have now. You have the love of many, and you shall always be remembered."

Then Jesus looked down at the slowly dying fire, added a few twigs to make the flame grow brighter, and said: "Memories are like this flame. We must make them burn in our hearts to comfort and inspire us. To be able to remember is a gift. Memories are like stars. They come to us when life seems dark to cheer us."

☙

The Effects of Anger

Jesus was perturbed at his followers' anger. He did not like to see them this way, and yet, he knew their anger was justified. What the rabbi had done was wrong.

"He teaches in the temple," Judas complained. "He explains what is written in the scriptures, but what does he do? And he . . . "

Peter interrupted Judas and said, "Yes, you might expect something like that to happen to one of us, but the man who committed this grave sin is a man of great knowledge."

Each and every one of them interjected his own thoughts and feelings.

There was sadness on Jesus' face and a bit of disappointment also showed through when he said: "My friends, anger has overtaken you. The anger has made you this way, but who are you to condemn?"

Matthew looked at Jesus, and there was anger in his eyes when he said: "He cursed me because I am a tax collector, he, the man who reads the scriptures, who knows better. He has committed a graver sin. Have you not always said, 'What belongs to Caesar is Caesar's and what belongs to God our Father is his alone, that we must separate the two, and yet we must live together in harmony'?" the other men grumbled in agreement.

Jesus replied, "This is true. But remember, he must face the shame he has brought on himself and feel the pain of a heavy heart, not you. Do not cast a stone at him to hurt him. He has already cast it himself. Yes, I know both of them, and they are in many ways good people. To condemn them is not for me, because I know I cannot be their judge. Again I say, they have condemned themselves, for they must live with their sin."

John said, "And she carries his child. Then that child . . . "— and he shook his head and could say no more.

Jesus said, "Have pity on the child, for the child is innocent."

Peter responded, "But the sins of the father are carried to his sons and their sons and their sons."

Jesus said, "The shame, yes, but the sin, no." Jesus continued, "Come, my friends, remember, would we want to be in such a position, any of us? Again I tell you, do not cast the first stone. Look into your own hearts and the wrongs you have done. Would you want someone to expose your sins and cast a stone at you?"

And then all at once, like a soft breeze, the anger in the men's faces turned into thoughtfulness as they began to review their own lives. Jesus said, "See, be just, but also be loving; be kind, but also be just. Do not do what you know is wrong, but do not be quick in judging others either."

❧

A Peaceful and Rewarding Day

Jesus had eaten with his friends, who now sat with him among the trees in an orchard. It had been a peaceful and rewarding day. His followers were as content as Jesus was. Peter said, "Master, don't you wish life could be this way every day—that we could eat to our hearts' content, enjoy good conversation, and rest afterward in an orchard?"

Jesus smiled and answered: "Yes, that would be nice. But Peter, we have much to do for the Father, and it would not be good for us—or anyone else—to enjoy ourselves each and every day."

"What?" John said.

Jesus cleared his throat and said: "You were dozing, John. I thought that would awaken you."

Everybody began to laugh and Jesus said, "There is work to be done in the fields. Such work is good. And there is the work of the mind. That is good work too. The body and mind should work together. We must be teachers, but we must also be doers and thinkers."

The men nodded to one another. Jesus continued: "If no one works in the fields, who will gather the wheat so that bread may be baked? If the women do not have wheat, they cannot bake bread. Life is like a chain. We are attached to one another until we are called home. We influence each and every person. We influence one another by our thoughts, our words, and our actions."

Then Jesus got up, touched the branch of a tree, and said: "There is always new life around us, but we who are older must strengthen this life as the trunk strengthens this tree. It gives life to the young branches, and the young branches give life to the fruit." Then he looked down and saw a small insect crawling upon the ground. He scooped it up, let it crawl on his hand, and said: "In many ways we are like this little bug as it searches for food and shelter. There are many peoples upon the earth, but we are one to my Father. He knows us, sees us, and understands us." And then, as gently and as quickly as he had picked up the bug, he placed it down on the earth.

The men looked at one another, and one of them began to laugh and said, "Master, tell me your dreams and what you want."

Jesus smiled once again and replied, "I wish there were peace among all peoples; that they would see wisdom in one another and would love one another; that they would understand all are equal in my Father's eye, that a child is a beautiful gift, that a woman is to be respected and honored, and that she in turn must honor and respect others; that the father, brother, and child are special, and that she wishes to make their life enjoyable; that she take pride in her baking and cooking; that the men who toil in the fields take pride when they carry wheat or pick fruit; that the merchant be pleased."

Then a sadness seemed to come over him like a sudden rainstorm, a tear slowly trickled from his eye, and he said, "My wish is that when our time comes, we will all return to the Father's loving home, that his arms be open to welcome us. But until that time, I wish for peace upon the earth, peace, peace, peace."

Male and Female, He Created Them

*J*esus' disciples sat around the fire, staring as if they expected to see it do something different. Jesus was with them, staring at the fire also.

"Master," Peter said breaking the silence, "the Father has created both males and females."

Jesus nodded in agreement.

Peter continued: "The male is the source from which we receive strength. Is this not what you have taught us, Master?"

Jesus nodded his head again.

"And the female is the source from which we draw love most fully. You have taught us that when strength and love are joined together, it is a gift as great as the sun. Master, is a woman truly that important in the Father's plan?"

Jesus sighed and answered: "I tell you this, my friend: Love is as important to the earth as water is. Without it, life could not exist. Love and strength together are a gift to fight pain, hatred, greed, and other forms of human evil." Peter threw two sticks on the fire while Jesus continued, "If man and woman work together, not only will they be able to bring new life to the earth, they will also be able to teach their children about God and his love."

John said: "I don't understand, Master."

Jesus replied: "Does not the fire burn more brightly because Peter has placed more wood on it?"

"Yes," John answered, "but that's natural. There's nothing strange about that."

Jesus smiled and asked, "And is it not natural for man and woman to work together, whether they are married or not, in order to make life better?"

Then Jesus looked down and said: "The Father created the earth for both man and woman, not man alone, for the woman is a part of the Father's love as are the sea, the sky, and the mountains."

A Rock and a Flower Are Alike

Jesus stooped to pick a flower growing among the rocks. John shook his head, expressing impatience. Simon said, "Doesn't he know we must be in town soon—that many people including the sick and the poor are waiting to hear his words?"

Judas complained: "Another teacher may be there before us, and they'll give their coins to him instead." He suddenly became silent when he realized that Jesus was watching and listening to the three of them.

"Shame," Jesus said, "shame. Do you not see the beauty in this flower?"

Peter said: "But surely, Master, you can understand our feelings. The faithful are waiting for you. The sick and the children hunger for your words. And besides, it is now the hottest part of the day, and you stop to pick a flower—not even a pretty one but one that grows among the rocks."

Jesus shook his head and said again: "Shame. Surely I have taught you better. You profess your love for my words."

"But . . . ," Peter responded.

"But nothing," Jesus interrupted. "Be silent."

Peter, like a dutiful student, became quiet and listened.

Jesus said: "The flowers blooming among the rocks are blue like the sky. And yet many people pass them by because they seem so common. A human being, a rock, and a flower are very much alike."

The disciples didn't want to laugh aloud, but they couldn't help snickering a bit. Jesus said: "Go ahead and laugh, my friends, if that is what you think about my words. When I came to earth, I was but a child. I have walked upon the earth, and now I am a man. But I still do not understand why people must so often act like the rock instead of the flower. All are equal in the eyes of my Father. Some are filled with strength and others with love. We are like a field of flowers. Each of us has a beauty of our own. But we do not take time to admire all of God's creation. We pluck this one out, ignore that one, and crush another one. In my Father's home, however, there is no prejudice. He made us different in the way we look, think, speak, and act, but we are all still like him."

When Jesus bent down again to pick some more flowers, Peter said, "Yes, maybe we are like a rock. A man came to me and cried out for help, but I refused him because he was not of our race."

Without looking up, Jesus said, "Remember, Peter, all are equal in my Father's eyes." Then he touched a leaf and a petal, looked up into the sky, and prayed: "Father, Father, like flowers we are tender, delicate, and crushable. Have pity on those who are oppressed, and guide those who oppress them to understand your will and to change their ways."

Smile

*I*t had been a long, difficult, hot day. The disciples sat around a small fire on a night turned cool and slowly ate the dry bread they had with them. Jesus began to smile, so much so that it appeared he was going to break into laughter. Peter noticed and said: "Master, how can you possibly smile at a time like this? I'm exhausted and worried. You have touched lepers, and the odor from that man who was badly burned was horrible."

Jesus looked at him and said, "You should smile."

"And what about that man who spit on you, Master?" John said. "All you did was try to comfort him with your words."

"You should smile," Jesus said again.

The disciples shook their heads in disbelief, and Judas said: "And what about the rich man who merely thanked you and gave you only one coin when he could afford to give many more? All you did was smile at him. How could you do that, Master? And now here you are smiling again even though we are totally exhausted, our feet ache, and we have nothing to eat but some dry bread we've been carrying around for a long time."

Jesus said: "You must smile."

"Smile at what?" they asked in unison.

Jesus answered: "Because you have life, because you have seen people healed, because you have received words of wisdom from my Father. But all you do is complain about your tired feet and your lack of food. Let us eat the bread as if it were a feast. And let us smile because we can still breathe in the fresh air, we can still see the sun setting, and we can hear the sounds of nature. There is joy in the world."

"But what about all the suffering, the hatred, and the destruction we've seen?" Peter asked.

Jesus raised his hands to the heavens and prayed aloud: "Father, they do not see your gifts in the world. Yes, there is suffering, and it pains my heart, but I can still see the beauty in nature and in humankind. I know from it that you love us so much."

The men around the campfire began to feel guilt as they looked at one another. But then slowly each smiled and then began to laugh until it sounded like a loud roar. Jesus said, "See, do you not feel better now?"

They smiled at one another, and Jesus was happy. He said: "We need smiling faces and happy hearts to tell the Father we know he has given us so much even though it seems so little at times."

↷

Listen to Yourself

The walk had been long and tiring. Jesus' friends were exhausted, hungry, and soaked to the skin from a downpour of rain that had stopped as quickly as it had started. Now there was no movement in the air, which was heavy with heat.

Peter said: "Let's rest. My legs won't carry me any farther."

John nodded in agreement and said: "Master, we must rest for awhile. We are tired and weary."

Jesus smiled, "Yes, my friends, sometimes I forget that the legs of fishermen are not as strong as the legs of those who work in the fields."

After they had rested for a while, Jesus broke the bread they had, and they began to eat. When they were finished, Peter said: "As tired as I am, I would love to soak my feet; they ache so much. When I was on my boat I would hang them over the side in the water."

John said, "But how could your feet be tired when all you did was sit all day and watch the fish swim into your nets?"

Peter began to laugh because he knew John was teasing him.

"It has been a long day," Jesus said, interrupting them. "We all want to rest now, but Peter wants to find a puddle of water to soak his tired feet."

Suddenly another storm came upon them. The peaceful silence was shattered as the wind and rain whipped the leaves on the trees. "Listen," Jesus said.

"Listen to what?" they asked. "It's raining, and who wants to listen to rain? It always makes the same sound."

In response Jesus said again, "Listen, my friends, listen."

"To what?" they asked again.

A hush fell over them as the rain beat in fury on the already soaked earth. The branches seemed to compete with the leaves to make the most noise. But then there was a flash of lightning followed by a crack of thunder. They were soaked to the skin for the second time that day.

When the storm passed and the rain stopped, Peter asked, "Master, what were we supposed to learn other than what it is like to feel miserable?"

Jesus answered, "There is so much to learn from listening, even listening to nature." And then he looked at his muddy and rain-soaked cloak, began to wring water from the hem, and said, "If we listened to one another as well as we listen to ourselves, we would better understand not only one another but also the universe."

The Gift of Knowing Right and Wrong

The men sat around the campfire, trying to warm their tired and weary bones. Jesus looked at those he had selected as his disciples and those who had come to hear him teach. Joy filled and warmed his tired body because he could see their great strength and because he knew they had been handpicked by the Father to accompany him and to live according to the Father's will.

Jesus listened as they spoke quietly to one another. It was John who spoke up and said, "Master, the others have selected me to ask you something."

Jesus responded: "What is wrong with them? Have their tongues stopped working?"

They all began to smile and laugh because they knew Jesus was teasing them.

Then Jesus asked, "Am I so unapproachable?"

"No," John answered, "but I hope I can put it in the right words so that you don't misunderstand what we're trying to say." Jesus smiled a small, knowing smile as John continued, "Master, for as long as we have followed you, none of us has ever heard you condemn or criticize, nor have we ever seen you walk away from someone who would not accept your beliefs."

Jesus nodded in agreement, and then there was silence for a while.

Finally, Peter said: "Master, you treat everyone the same, whether the person is a fisherman, a farmer, a woman who bakes bread, or a child who begs at the gate. You always show kindness and concern to everyone, even to the rich merchant or the tax collectors we all hate."

Jesus replied: "There are many jewels here on earth in my Father's kingdom. Each one shines in its own way, and each has its own value. Each soul is a jewel because it has been given life by my Father. One may seem precious to some people but not to others. However, in my Father's eyes they are all precious, even though some may shine more brilliantly because of their kindness, caring, love, and understanding.

That is because they listen for his voice, look for his presence, and try to do his work so that there may be peace and joy on earth."

Peter said, "Master, you see in us what we do not see in ourselves."

Jesus answered: "I can only repeat the words my Father gives to me. I cannot change what he tells me, but we all have free will. Remember, my friends, that each soul has been given the gift of knowing what is right and what is wrong."

A Bouquet of Wildflowers

Jesus was gathering wildflowers in a field near the road. Peter, Judas, and John stood and shook their heads. "I do not understand the Master," Peter said. "Why is he stopping to pick flowers? Why is it so important to him? We have a long journey ahead of us, and he is holding us back." John also seemed perturbed at what Jesus was doing. But Jesus, humming to himself, carefully gathered the blue and yellow flowers. Then suddenly he straightened his back, looked up to the sky, and raised the bouquet of wildflowers as if he were giving it to someone they could not see.

Judas said: "The Master has been working much too long." And he cried out, "Master, let's go." Jesus did not answer.

"Master," John cried. But Jesus still seemed lost in thought. Slowly the flowers began to fall from his hand.

This time it was Peter who said, "Now I know it is time for the Master to rest." He hurriedly ran into the field.

Jesus turned and said, "My friends, why are you so concerned about me?"

"Master, don't you know what you just did? You picked some wildflowers, you raised them up to heaven as if you were lost in a dream, and then you let them fall from your hand. Is this a normal way for someone to act?" Peter asked.

Jesus smiled and answered: "My friends, why does it concern you? Is it wrong to pick flowers and offer their beauty to the Father?"

The three men looked at one another, embarrassed.

Then Judas said: "Master, why didn't you let them grow? Why did you have to pick them and make them die? Why couldn't you share their beauty with others?"

A beautiful smile filled Jesus' face and he said: "You are learning well, my friend, but just as all must feel life, so too all must feel death. These flowers in another day would have shriveled and died. But I picked them and offered up their beauty before that happened."

"Well, why didn't you pick the ones that are going to die today?" Judas asked.

Jesus answered, "Would you offer them to the Father?"

Judas said nothing but turned and slowly began to walk away.

"Stop," Jesus said. "Come here. There is a lesson to learn. When you pray"—and he looked at each one of them in turn—"do you offer your prayers with hope? Thoughtful prayers, prayers that are sincere and filled with love? That is what I did when I offered the Father the flowers he has created."

Then Jesus bent down and picked up three blue and three yellow wildflowers that had fallen upon the earth, and he gave a yellow and a blue one to each of them. They looked at the flowers, which were beginning to wilt. John said, "Master, why did you give these to us? Why didn't you pick new flowers?"

Jesus looked at them and said: "Maybe this is the kind of gift you give to the Father. Do you truly speak to him with love and caring as you would to another? Or do you speak to him as if there is no one there because you cannot see him? Speak with your heart, my sons. Speak with your heart, with your mind, and with the beauty in your soul." Then he slowly raised both of his hands to the heavens and said: "Father, I thank you for all that you have given to the earth. Let it be strengthened with your love. Give to all a blessing that we may do your will with love, caring, and sharing."

Jesus Teaches the Crowds

Respect for God's Word

A wise man traveled many miles to visit the man called Master and Healer. He was disappointed as he approached Jesus, but he tried not to allow it to show in his tired eyes or in his voice. His servant went up to Jesus first and said: "My master wishes to speak to you. Will you see him?"

Jesus smiled and answered: "I already see him. Tell him to come close."

The old man slowly walked closer. Jesus asked, "Who are you, and why have you come to see me?"

There was silence for a few moments before the old man answered: "I wish to speak with you because I have heard so much about you. That's why I have come looking for you."

Jesus said, "Come, enter my home." And he bade the old man to sit down under the shade of a tree. The old man didn't expect this. Who was this man who asked him to enter a home he didn't have? But still, there was something in Jesus' voice that commanded respect and love.

Jesus said: "You have come to question me for you wonder about my knowledge. It is very simple and basic." The old man nodded. Jesus continued: "You are surprised that I am not dressed in fine clothes and that my home is open to everyone, for it belongs to no one and yet to everyone. You also question my power of healing. You expected to see great throngs of people hanging onto every word I speak, but there is only a small handful. I tell you this, my wise friend: What you have seen is all that you will see. My words are from my Father. They are simple and pure like running water."

The old man thought for a while and then said, "May I call you Master?"

Jesus nodded and the wise old man continued: "What you have said is true, but in many ways a simple word or action has more value than the finest gold. I have learned much from the poor, the sick, and those with troubled minds. In the same way, although you have not given them gold, your words have given them hope, wisdom, and strength."

Words from the Father

The scene was very serene—Jesus sitting on a rock, the smell of salt water in the air, the sand bleached almost white by the sun, and men of every age listening intently as he spoke convincingly about the importance of loving, caring, and sharing. "These are the words of my Father, not mine," Jesus proclaimed.

A wise old man who sat among them was surprised by the wisdom of such a young man. He said to Jesus, "You are called Master."

"Yes," Jesus answered. "I am a teacher."

The wise old man replied: "A teacher? How long have you studied the scriptures?"

Jesus responded, "It comes to me like the flow of the waves, the heat of the sun, the light from the stars."

And then a young man strolled over and sat on a rock close to Jesus. He asked, "Who are you?"

Jesus answered: "Have I not told you? Is it really that important? Is not my message more important than who I am? Is not my message believable?"

The young man turned to the other men and said: "We have all listened to him for hours, but only two of us have asked him questions. Have you no questions to ask? Are you simply going to listen to him and blindly accept whatever he says?"

One man spoke up and said: "I find no fault with what he teaches, for he speaks from the heart. Is this so wrong?"

Another said: "He is only the son of a carpenter. What does he know? He even claims that his message comes from his Father."

Jesus raised his hand and said: "The Father I speak of is the Father of us all."

There was a great deal of grumbling when he said this. Jesus looked out to the sea and said: "When you see the beauty and power of nature, can you deny that there is a higher power—a Creator? Is nature something that we just thought up? Many times we have problems just sowing seeds!" And then he touched the rock on which he was sitting and said, "It is strong, is it not?"

One of the men responded, "Yes, but if we roll it down the hill, we can break it."

Jesus replied: "Yes, what you say is true, and words can be broken too. But can nature be destroyed completely? Can we drain the seas dry? And if we could, what would we do with it? Where would we put it—in our pocket? Can we remove all the mountains? Where would we put them—in the valleys? We must eat and drink if we are to survive. But we must also listen to the words of the Father, for they sustain the life in our soul."

The men grumbled among themselves. Jesus just sat there as if he were alone on an island. Finally, another man spoke up, "I respect you, but I do not believe that you truly are the son of the Father."

Jesus responded: "It is good to respect others. You must freely choose what you will believe, but you must have an open mind. You have listened well to all that I have said for many days. You will think about my words, and then you will make your own decision. Who I am does not concern you now, but when the time comes for you to be called home again, you will be grateful that you knew me."

"What do you mean?" another man in the crowd asked.

"I cannot explain these words now," Jesus answered, "just as you cannot explain why people must eat and drink."

A man began to laugh and said: "If we do not eat or drink, we die."

Jesus said in response, "And if you do not follow the rules of my Father, what do you think will happen to you when your time comes to return to my Father's home?" Again there was mumbling among them.

Jesus looked up to heaven and said: "Father, forgive them and strengthen them. I know they believe in you from the questions they ask me. Do not let them see the pain I feel in my heart. Let them hear only your word. And let me be your instrument to bring peace and love to the world."

A young boy who had been silent came up to Jesus, extended his hands to him, and said, "Master, will you listen to me?"

Jesus looked down at the child and answered, "Yes, I listen to all."

The young boy said: "I believe what you say, but I do not understand why you were put on the earth. What are you here for?"

Jesus smiled and replied: "For such a young man, there is much wisdom in you." He continued: "Remember my words, son, remember my words. We are all instruments of the Father. We are all his children, and we must pass his words on to the children to come so that they are never forgotten, never changed. They must always be present like the earth, the sea, and the sun in the sky." Then he hugged the young man.

Words Open Hearts and Minds

For four days a young man camped near Jesus' group. Even though Peter asked him to join them, he refused. After the fourth day, as the crowd disbursed, Jesus approached the young man and said: "You have not asked a single question, but you stare at me intently. You seem to take in my words as dry soil soaks up every drop of rain.

The young man nodded and replied: "I did not want to refer to you as Master. I did not even want to come to hear you, but my mother, who is a good woman, begged me, and I could not refuse her. I have been inspired by you. There are many questions I wanted to ask, but I didn't."

"Why not?" Jesus asked.

The young man shook his head and answered: "At first I thought the men and women were only asking questions you wanted and prepared them to ask, but I have seen their hearts and minds open to your love and to your Father's words. When I return home, I pray that I will be able to speak as you do and properly instruct those in our small village with the Father's words. But a part of me is frightened."

Jesus said: "My son, when you repeat the Father's words, speak them from your heart and mind. It is important to speak this way. Also fast and pray, and the words will flow like a river. Enlighten like a star in the night those who see only darkness. Share with them the light you have received. Go now in peace and remember that you will never be alone, even though many may mock you or even throw stones at you. It is not an easy path when you walk the path of righteousness and speak the words of the Father. My arms shall always be around your heart. My words will be embedded in your heart and mind like stones on the road of life. You may stumble, but you will always know that you are loved."

Preserving God's Words

Jesus watched a young man unroll some parchment. His head was bent, and he began to write as soon as Jesus began to speak. When he looked up, it was easy to see the frustration on his face. Jesus continued to speak to the crowd, healing, inspiring, and giving the Father's love to all those gathered around him.

When Jesus finished speaking, the young man was still writing. Peter said, "Master, you should talk slower."

Turning to Peter, Jesus said, "Why?"

Peter answered: "Master, don't you understand? Didn't you see?"

"See what?" Jesus asked, teasing Peter.

He answered: "Master, you know what I mean. How is the word to get out? He is writing."

"To whom?" Jesus asked.

"Well, I didn't ask him," Peter said. "Do you want me to?"

Jesus placed his hand on Peter's shoulder and answered, "Be patient, my friend, be patient."

Jesus walked over to where the young man was still writing on the parchment and said: "I see you are busy. What are you writing?"

The young man answered, "This is something I want to do, and I'm even being paid to do it."

"And . . . ?" Jesus said.

"And," the young man said, "I know your words must be preserved for all to hear."

"Do you believe in me?" Jesus asked.

The young man sighed and answered: "I know what I have seen. I know what I have heard. But I'm not sure."

"So be it, my friend," Jesus said, "but it is not necessary to write every word, for much of what has been given to me by my Father will be carried by word of mouth, but only a few words of what I have just spoken, only a very few."

Then he placed his hand on the young man's shoulder and said: "Remember this, my friend, you are blessed and you are loved. Go your way. Collect your coin. But remember my words in your heart. For the time will come when the pen will no longer be used."

The young man got up, Jesus turned, and each went his own way.

Plain Words

A man approached Jesus and said, "Master, I have recorded many of your words."

Jesus said: "It is not wrong for you to write them down, but it is wrong for you to give them a different meaning. Why have you done this, my son?"

The man stammered a little bit, trying to think of a way to defend himself. "Master," he said finally, "you speak in parables that many of us don't understand, even when we read the words over and over again. We interpret them in one way, and they seem right. We interpret them in another way, and they seem wrong."

Jesus said: "I assure you that the words my Father speaks through me are plain enough. Only when listeners distort them do they become confusing, because they refuse to believe. My Father has given you a great gift, enabling you to bring new life by introducing truth and inspiration and laughter to situations where there is no life. *Strength* and *sensitivity* and *love* and *compassion* are words, but they can be more than words. They can actually be expressed and come alive in the speaking. I tell you this: Never use words in such a way that you close the door of my Father's home to any of his children. It would be better to be born deaf, dumb, and blind than to use my Father's gifts to hurt one of his children."

Everlasting Words

A fter Jesus had finished teaching the small group of people gathered around him, a young man said: "Master, your words have inspired us but we are so few in number. How can you claim that your Father's words will travel across the earth like mighty rivers, be heard in all languages, and be spoken, heard, and felt by all? How can this be so?"

Jesus seemed to be very tired as he sat down and said: "I tell you this: My Father's words will last forever. Do the rains ever cease to fall?"

One person quickly answered, "No, Master."

But an older man who was considered to be wise added, "There are times when there is very little rain, Master."

"That is true," Jesus said, "but eventually it appears, does it not?"

"Yes," the wise man said.

Jesus said: "My Father's words will live as long as there are those to hear them. Even when we cease to walk the earth, the Father's words will still be heard in the heavens. We, his children, are gifts to all and so are his words. They will be recorded on scrolls, in the sand, and on stone. By word of mouth they shall be spoken to the young and to the old, passed from person to person and from age to age. Everyone who wishes to hear them will be given the opportunity."

When all but a few of his disciples had departed, Jesus looked at the marks they had left from sitting and standing upon the earth. He began to smooth them over with his hands. Then he made an imprint of his own hand in the soft soil. Peter watched and said nothing, but then his curiosity got the better of him and he asked, "Master, what are you doing?"

Jesus said: "People are changeable, like the earth, Peter. One makes a mark, and then others come along and cover it over or erase it and leave their own marks. I tell you that no one will truly know and feel the power of my Father's words until the end."

Sacred Words

Three wise men of great learning came to visit Jesus and to ask him many questions. With love and respect he answered each of them by calling upon the wisdom of his Father and giving his words to them. One of the three asked him, "Master, should everyone make pilgrimages to learn from those who have studied the Father's words and can speak them, even though such a journey is long, tiring and unsafe?"

Jesus looked at the young man and said, "You have already made such a visit in coming to see me and question me, have you not?"

The young man snickered and said: "But we have found such simple surroundings here. We were expecting to find you in a temple."

Jesus responded: "I tell you this: My Father's word is sacred whether it is spoken in the desert, in the wilderness, in a humble home, or in a palace of stone built with the greatest of care. Comfort and knowledge comes from the one who teaches the Father's words and not from the place in which that person speaks them. Those who have made such a journey filled with hardship shall be enlightened in soul by my Father's words, even though their body and mind are tired. I cannot speak for everyone, but I can speak for myself. And I tell you that there is love in my Father's home for those who make an effort to know and understand his words, to learn as much as they can about them. One only has to look around to see my Father's love. But in order to hear his words, a person must go to another who has heard them and wants to share them."

A woman who was tired and worn-looking said to Jesus, "Master, I'd like to know how I can be healed."

Jesus looked at her and said, "I cannot see any illness in your body."

She responded: "That's not what I meant. I want to know how the words of the Father can heal my mind and soul."

Jesus smiled and answered: "Woman, you have taken the first step to receiving the key of knowledge. There is power in the words of my Father that can heal the body, mind, and soul. Pain and suffering may still touch the life of those who seek to know his words and live by his rules, but they will know in their heart and soul that they do not walk alone in life. My Father has given us rules to guide us and heal us. In his love he has given us the earth and so much more. Because of his love there will always be hope. But we must first open our heart and mind if we are to experience this love and hope."

Then Jesus looked up and added, "Then and only then will he who has the key of knowledge to the heavens come again."

Writing God's Words

*J*esus was pleased to see among those following him one day a scholar who was well known and respected. They greeted one another, and the man said, "I am pleased to be with you."

"And I am happy to see you," Jesus said with a smile. "Come and sit with me."

They sat down and the scholar said: "Master, I have a question for you. I have a great desire to write about you and your friends, to write about what I see, think, and feel. I don't know where this desire comes from, but at times it seems to be a gift and at times a curse."

"My friend"—Jesus reached out and touched his hand—"it is good that you want to do this, for many have been given great talents to work in the fields, to care for the animals, to build, to do carpentry, to teach, to write, and to record. Without the gift of writing, my words and the word of the Father could not be recorded."

The young scholar was happy because Jesus was pleased with him. Jesus smiled and said: "Write so that people may understand. Be honest and truthful. Do not lie. The words you write shall last and be interpreted many times in different ways. But I tell you this: In the end the truth shall be seen for what it is. The word will be there for all to hear, see, and know. Its meaning will no longer be hidden or misinterpreted."

Unforgotten Words

It was a quiet morning. The sun was just beginning to peak through the clouds. Jesus felt renewed because he had slept well that night. He took a deep breath of fresh, clean air and looked at his disciples, who were still sound asleep. He smiled like a proud father looking at his children, for these men had given up much to follow him, especially Peter, who was older than the others. Jesus remembered the many stories they had told him. Some of them were just beginning to live, while the lives of others were coming to an end.

Jesus began to walk, slowly humming to himself because this day was beginning well. A man sitting near a tree said, "Good morning, Master."

"Good morning," Jesus said in return. "It looks as if it is going to be a good day."

"Yes," the man said. Then he added, "I didn't want to bother you last night, and so I have been waiting here for you."

"You should have come closer where the fire could have warmed you," Jesus said.

"No," the man said. "I just wanted to sit here and watch and listen."

Jesus asked, "Did you hear or see anything that pleased you?"

The man answered, "Master, I heard your disciples say how much they love you."

"Yes, I know this," Jesus said. "They are good men who try to do what my Father teaches them."

The man looked at Jesus and asked, "Master, will people remember your words?"

"My friend," Jesus said, "each day of life is a new beginning because my Father gives us love that we can hold in our heart like a tiny seed. When we teach, care for, or comfort another, we share that love. Every day of our life we should teach, learn, and love. We need only to look and we will see my Father's love all around us. I tell you this, my friend: My words will be recorded for all to hear because they are the words of my Father and will not be forgotten. However, many times they will be misunderstood and interpreted in a way I did not intend. People may try to change my Father's rules, but my words are binding and cannot be erased."

Words That Make God Present

A man followed Jesus for nearly three months, listening closely but never saying much. One day he extended his hand to Jesus and said: "Master, I have walked with you, eaten with you, and stayed with you. Your words are so beautiful because they have power to open our minds." Jesus seemed pleased with his complement because he knew this man was well schooled in the words of his Father. The man continued: "I have studied with many masters and read many books filled with great inspiration and wisdom, but I tell you this, Master—and I am proud to address you as such—you speak as if the Father is right here with us, guiding our very lives, if only we call out to him and ask him to open our minds and inspire us."

Jesus nodded in agreement and said, "I think you understand that the words I speak are not always my own."

"Then they should be recorded. I should be writing all that you have taught us," the man said.

Jesus smiled at his enthusiasm and concern, and said: "I tell you this: You will remember my words as will others. But they are like the flowers that bloom; everyone does not experience their beauty at the same time. One does not drink the green wine but waits until it has matured. My words, like flowers, do not all bear fruit. Like seeds, some fall on fertile soil, some in the crevice of a rock, and others on the rock itself. The sunlight will touch, kiss, and warm only some of them. The same happens to my words as they are placed in a person's mind. There is no need, then, to sit and record them, for many will remember them.

"Children may not remember the words their mother spoke to them when they were ill and cared for by her, but they will never forget their mother's warmth and love. And the mother remembers those times as well—not her tiredness, but her love for her child. And so, fear not, my friend, fear not that all of my words have not been recorded."

Love One Another

Jesus Learns from His Mother

The woman's face was bony, drawn, and wrinkled. Begging, she would cry out in the streets: "For my children! For my children!" Occasionally someone would give her a coin. Usually it was a Roman soldier, even though she was neither Roman nor Jew.

Jesus asked: "Mother, why does she cry out in our streets? Why doesn't she go to her own people and ask them to help her?"

Mary looked at Jesus and said: "I don't know, my son. Maybe she thinks she'll collect more coins here, maybe she knows more people here, or maybe they're poorer than we are."

"Why are you going to give her some of our sticks?" Jesus asked.

"So that she may build a fire to make her bread," Mary answered.

"But mother, where will she get the grain or the flour?"

"She will find it," Mary said.

"But all she does is beg, Mother."

Mary smiled and said, "My son, that is work."

"Is it honorable work?" Jesus asked. "And if it is, why do you not go into the streets and beg?"

Mary looked at her son, almost disapprovingly, and said: "Because I don't have to. Your father provides enough for us."

"But we would have more, Mother."

Mary looked at her son in disbelief and said, "My son, do you not have enough bread to eat?"

"Yes, Mother, but there are times I would like more."

Mary began to smile and said, "My son, my friend."

"My friend?" Jesus asked, and he began to laugh.

"Yes, my son and my friend," she said. "Like the sun and the sky, you are usually bright, but sometimes you are like the night. No matter how many times I try to explain something to you, you do not see the light. This woman is to be pitied and yet admired, for it is not easy to cry out in the streets."

When they approached the woman, she recognized them.

"Have you done well today?" Mary asked her. She didn't answer, and so Mary said, "My friend, you complain all the time."

The woman smiled and said, "I have many mouths to feed."

Mary said, "You wouldn't have so many if you didn't take in so many."

The woman said, "I know, but I can't leave them wandering hungry in the streets."

Mary said: "You are doing so much good, but why do you bring together children who are lame, lonely, and filled with sorrow and pain?"

"I don't know, Mary," the woman answered, "but I know there's a quickening in my heart when I do, and then a strange mixture of joy and sorrow when they leave."

Jesus touched the woman and said, "Woman, you shall be blessed by my Father."

The woman began to laugh and said, "The son of a carpenter, and he talks like a man in the temple."

Mary's face radiated pride as she said, "Woman, you pay me a great compliment, but I only pray that he takes up his father's trade."

Jesus smiled and said, "Mother, I have already begun."

The smile quickly faded from Mary's face, her heart grew as heavy as stone, and she said, "Not yet my son, for you are only twelve."

"I have begun, Mother," Jesus said. "I have begun."

How to Show Love

While Jesus stood near the entrance to the temple, an older man who was thought to be very wise stared long and hard into his eyes, almost without blinking. Then he said, aware of Jesus' reputation, "Throughout my many years I can't even begin to count the number of people who have tried to change my way of thinking, but none of them has been a match for my wisdom and intelligence."

Jesus just listened and said nothing, refusing to be baited into an argument as to who was wiser or more intelligent.

Finally the wise old man challenged Jesus: "If I ask you a question, will you give me an answer?"

Jesus said, "It may not be to your liking, but yes, I will answer you."

The wise old man thought for a while and then asked: "What is love? And what is the best way to show it?"

Jesus thought for a long time. The wise old man stared at him, his expression never changing, almost as if he were trying to distract Jesus or put pressure on him. "You are taking a very long time, my friend," he said.

Jesus smiled gently and said: "You have called me a friend. That is one way of showing love to another."

The wise old man broke into a smile and he dropped his attitude of superiority, for he knew that he had never met anyone like this before.

However, he wasn't so much in awe of Jesus' quick and perceptive mind that he couldn't point out, "But you really haven't answered my question fully."

"Come and sit with me," Jesus said. Then Jesus said: "Your sitting with me is a form of caring. When we take time to visit another, is that not a form of love?"

The wise old man laughed to himself and then said, "You have tricked me into answering my own question."

"No, I have not tricked you," Jesus said. "It was you who called me your friend, and it was you who decided to sit with me when I invited you."

Yes, the wise old man thought to himself, but it won't ever happen again! And he waited patiently to analyze closely every word Jesus spoke, but Jesus said nothing. Finally the wise old man broke the silence and said, "You stare into the heavens but have nothing to say about your searching."

Jesus said: "Friendship—that is, caring and loving—is often best expressed in silence. Is this not true?"

The man extended his hand to Jesus and said, "Master."

"Again, you have answered your own question," Jesus said. "For now you have given to me what my Father has given to you. That is what we are here to do—to care for, to respect, and to love one another. You have spent many hours and days in the temple. What have you received from my Father?"

The wise old man stared in amazement at Jesus, who had turned the tables on him, and said, "I have received wisdom and an inner peace."

"Then you have received a silent but powerful love from him, and those who follow in my footsteps will receive silent love from both my Father and me. Love is the care that we receive from my Father and then share with others, giving to them the great gifts of friendship, caring, and respect. I tell you that my Father cares for each of us from the moment of conception until our soul reaches his gates when he calls us home again.

Jesus got up and gently but firmly pulled the wise old man to his feet. They kissed each other on both cheeks. Then Jesus said, "My friend, we shall meet again, but then there shall be no age difference between us."

The old wise man understood and said, "Master, I eagerly await that meeting."

Caring for One Another

Mary Magdalene saw an old woman sitting alone by the side of the road and stopped because the woman seemed troubled. "Come with me," Mary said to her, "and my Master will give you something to eat and drink." She helped the woman to get to her feet, and the woman slowly and painfully walked with her.

After they had walked quite a distance, the woman asked Mary Magdalene: "Why did you stop to help me? No one else did."

Mary simply said, "I'm going to see the Master, and I'm sure he'd like to meet you."

Mary was filled with joy when she spotted Jesus in the distance. But the old woman hesitated and asked, "Why would he want to see me?"

"Why not?" Mary answered.

When they reached the spot where Jesus was standing with Peter, Luke, and John, Jesus said, "Woman, eat some bread and drink some wine with us."

When she was finished, sadness replaced the satisfaction in her eyes and she said, "I must leave now."

"Why?" Mary Magdalene asked. "You can stay with me in my home," she added, knowing that the old woman had no place to live.

"No, I don't want to," she said.

"Tell her to come with me," Mary said to Jesus.

He put his hand on Mary's shoulder, as if to comfort her, and said: "Woman, woman, do you not understand? Some must stay close to the shelter of the home or even hide within it. Others must wander with no home to call their own."

"But she'll die," Mary objected. "No one will take care of her."

Jesus smiled and said: "Mary, there are many good people who will share what they have with her. She wishes to be lost among the crowds of people in the city and to be a loner upon the road."

To the woman Jesus said: "Woman, go in peace. I shall be with you until you reach your home."

"But, Master," Peter said, "she has no home. Is this not so?"

"Yes," Jesus said, "she has no home in this world, but in my Father's home she will be welcomed."

Then Jesus said to Mary: "I tell you this: Do not force your ways on others, for your ways and their ways may not be the same. Be kind, gentle, understanding, and share what you have with them. But love should not be forced. Its gentleness can open their hearts and minds. Yet if they feel only its strength, they may turn away from your efforts."

A Child Delights Jesus

A young boy approached Jesus and said, "Master, I have been told that you are very wise."

"Now, who told you that, my child?"

With wonder and amazement in both his eyes and voice, the young boy said, "They say you know everything, Master."

"Everything?" Jesus said. "No, my son. No one knows everything. But I'll try to answer your questions as well as I can. Come and sit next to me."

Jesus was pleased by the gentleness and innocence he saw in the boy's eyes, and he thought about his own childhood. How nice it was then. He hoped that he had given the same amount of love and joy to his father that this young child was giving to him now. The boy asked: "Master, in the temple we say 'Shalom.' What does it really mean?"

Jesus answered: "Shalom is a giving. It is the kind of giving a newborn receives when placed at the breast of his mother to suck until the milk flows. It is the kind of giving children provide for an aged, dying parent who wishes to return home again by calling upon my Father to take and receive that parent with love. It is the kind of giving a young widow with children receives when she does not know where the next crust of bread will come from, and someone knocks on her door and gives her wheat to make bread."

Then the young boy asked, "What does your Father think about us?"

"My Father feels only peace for us," Jesus said.

"Does he not understand how much suffering we've caused here on earth?" the boy asked.

"Yes, he knows," Jesus said. "But he knows and feels things in a different way than you and I do. Father, mother, and child can all look at the same thing and see and feel it differently."

"Come," Jesus said and he stretched out his hands. The boy took his cue and placed his hands in the firm grasp of the Master. "If I hold your hands tightly," Jesus said, "you cannot strike me, but if I loosen my grip, you can."

"Oh, no, Master, I would never hit you; I have no reason to be angry with you," the young boy said, horrified.

"But others will, my son," Jesus said, "others will. Many do not like to be restrained by others or by my Father. They want to be free as a bird. But I tell you this: There will not be peace if people refuse to follow the rules that my Father designed to prevent the growth of war from hatred and greed."

The young boy got up, bent down, and kissed Jesus first on the left cheek and then on the right. Jesus smiled and returned the kiss.

"Shalom, Master," the young boy said.

"Shalom, my friend," Jesus said. "And when you come upon people who are fighting, cry out 'Shalom' to them. If they do not hear you, cry it out louder. If they still refuse to listen, take their hands, clasp them to one another, and place your own hands over theirs until the bitterness and anger are gone. Then wish them peace and tell them to live once again according to my Father's words. His rules are difficult but not impossible."

A Good Samaritan

It seemed as if Jesus had been walking for days, so tired and worn did he look. Peter and Judas were with him when they heard a sound like moaning in the distance.

Judas said, "It's only the wind."

Peter disagreed. "It sounds like a person in terrible pain."

They stopped, and Judas said: "Let's go, Master. Don't waste time. They're waiting for you in the town."

Jesus looked at Judas and said, "Judas, be silent for a while."

The sound of moaning came once again through the silent trees.

"It's just the wind," Judas insisted.

"That's not the wind," Peter said, and he ran off in the direction of the moaning.

Jesus followed him, and they found a man who looked like a beggar—his clothes torn and dirty, his body beaten and bloody. He was clutching something tightly in his hands.

Jesus bent down and gently used the sleeve of his garment to wipe the man's face.

"Come, Master," Judas said. "You have no time for this." Jesus looked sternly at Judas, and, in a commanding way he seldom used, he said: "Be silent! I don't want to hear your voice."

As he lifted the beaten man's body and rested it against his shoulder, Jesus said, "Let me make you more comfortable."

The man looked up, trying to focus his swollen eyes, and asked through bleeding lips, "Are you the man they call Jesus of Nazareth?"

"Yes," Jesus answered.

"I have heard about you and have come to hear you speak," he said.

Judas started to say something but stopped when Jesus looked at him. Peter went to get a cloth and something to drink from the belongings they had dropped on the road. When he returned, he told the man, "This will make you feel better."

Again the man tried to focus his eyes on Jesus and asked, "Master, why have they done this to me?"

Jesus said sadly, "I can't tell you what causes people to hurt one another, for we are all children of my Father."

"Master, I wish to follow you," the man said.

Judas muttered under his breath, not daring to speak aloud, "How can he follow us? He's nothing but a beggar."

The man started to moan again, and so Jesus stayed with him throughout the night. When the sun began to rise, Peter said, "Master, aren't you tired from watching over him so long?"

"Yes," he said, "but we must care for one another. The love and caring we give will be returned many times."

Judas became excited then because he thought the Master meant that the man was wealthy after all and would reward them. Jesus just shook his head and said: "Judas, Judas, you don't have to speak the words. I know what's in your mind."

The man felt stronger and stood up when Jesus placed his hands on his forehead. He slowly opened his swollen fingers and offered Jesus a precious and beautiful stone. Jesus would not take it, but he nodded toward Peter and said, "Give it to him if you wish."

Judas became very angry and complained, "I'm the one who handles the money."

Jesus said: "Don't be selfish. This should be given to the temple where they truly love my Father and help his children who are in need."

Friendship

*J*esus sat by the edge of the water, which was cool and refreshing as the waves hit the rocks and splashed on him. "Come on, Master," Peter said, "It's time to go."

"Just a few more minutes," Jesus responded.

"But, Master," Peter complained, "your friends are waiting for you. Let's go or we'll be late."

Jesus smiled and said, "I am coming, Peter."

But as he stood, he tripped and fell head first into the water.

"Oh, Master," Peter exclaimed. "How clumsy you are!"

"Yes," Jesus responded, "that I am."

Peter realized what he had blurted out and apologized: "I'm sorry, Master. There was no reason for me to say that."

Jesus smiled again and said: "That is all right, Peter. You only stated what you felt."

Peter replied: "I want you to understand, Master, that I was concerned because your friends are waiting for you. I'm sure the bread is baked, and the wine is ready."

Jesus asked: "Peter, Peter, are you thinking more of the food or of my friends?"

"Don't get me wrong, Master," Peter answered. "Of course I'll be happy to see our friends, but I am hungry. You must excuse me, because food often comes first now that I'm getting a little older."

Jesus laughed and said: "Peter, Peter, friendship is the most important type of food. It is a filling, a giving, and a sharing. If we have a true friend, we will never be alone. If we have but one friend, we are blessed. And even if that friend dies before us, the memories of the time spent with that person will be like the sun to brighten our day."

Peter said, "Master, I have a friend in you."

Jesus responded, "I have a friend in you, too."

And then Jesus looked down at his wet clothes. In fact, he was soaked to the skin. Even though the sun beat down upon him all along the way, he was still not completely dry when he reached the home of the merchant. Before entering, he looked up to the sky and said, "Thank you, Father, that it was only the waters of the sea that soaked me and not the tears of humanity."

Peter stopped and asked, "Master, what did you say?"

Jesus answered: "Peter, Peter, remember this. When I am gone, never forget that I shall in reality always be with you and with all. People only have to ask, and I will be at their side. But I can only enter a heart that is open to me."

The Need for Compassion

*J*esus was appalled at what he was seeing and cried out, "Stop, in the name of justice and love."

Peter quickly hobbled over to Jesus and said: "Be careful! They may turn on us."

Jesus called out again, "Stop!"

And the robbers ran away. They left behind a man who was bleeding and hurt. There were tears in his eyes as he looked up at Jesus and said, "Thank you." As Jesus bent down and wiped his soiled face, they immediately recognized one another. Jesus gave him something to drink, and the man again thanked him.

When the man was finished drinking, he said to Jesus, "We are so different from each other, and yet we both speak about the need to love and care for one another." Jesus nodded in agreement, and the man continued: "If you had let them beat me to death, you would have been the only one to teach in the city. The crowd would have been large, and you would have received many coins."

Jesus nodded and said: "My friend, there is much to be done in this world. Anyone who speaks about truth, caring, and love to those whose hearts are open will make the world better. I tell you this: Even though we may not agree on everything we teach, the same kindness, generosity, and caring are in our heart, mind, and soul. This world is so vast. There is a great need for compassion and a willingness to share. I tell you to go and teach. You are not an evil man but a man filled with love of the Father. You see and hear him in one way, and I see and hear him in another. A field of flowers may all appear to be the same, but if we look closely we will see that there is a difference, maybe very slight, in color, strength, and the new life springing forth from each. Go, my friend, and peace be with you."

Peter looked at Jesus and said, "Master, you have such great love in you."

Jesus replied, "Peter, should we not all be that way?"

A Man Overcome with Grief

Jesus stood up and asked, "Are there any more questions?"

One man said, "Master," then he hung his head and continued, "I am filled with shame. I do not know how to ask this."

Jesus said, "Do not be ashamed, for we are friends, are we not?"

The other men nodded in agreement as Jesus said, "Speak up so that we may learn from one another."

The man said: "My wife cries constantly. She eats only enough to stay alive, and she has lost interest in me and in our home. Our servants do as they please because she does not direct them.

Jesus asked, "Why do you think she is doing this?"

There was a long pause, and finally the man answered: "My wife lost our baby, a boy with whom I was well pleased. But the baby only lived a few hours. Remorse has overtaken her, and she is filled with guilt because she is not able to bear any more children. It was a male child, Master, one who would have taken my name as I took my father's."

Jesus extended his hand and said, "My friend, have you tried to comfort her?"

The man answered: "But, Master, you do not understand. I, too, am grief stricken."

Jesus looked at him with sadness in his eyes and said: "But it was your wife who carried the child, was it not? And when her body grew large, and it was time for the child to be born, did she not suffer and cry out? Her pain now is even harder to bear. It was your child, yes, but it was her love that gave life to the child with the blessing of the Father. When the child died, she felt unworthy because she could not give you another. But is not your love strong? Go to your wife and tell her you love her. Remember, there are many in your village who have no one to care for them. They have no shepherd. They are lost sheep. Help them, and you shall grow. Love them, and you shall feel comforted. Give to them, and you shall be blessed."

The man said: "A sickness in our village killed many people and left others alone without any family. But they are not of my flesh, Master. I will do what you say, but how can I love those who are not members of my family?"

Jesus looked at him once again, then turned and walked slowly toward a patch of wildflowers, picked one, turned, and said, "To whom do these belong?"

The man laughed and answered, "To no one, Master, to no one."

Jesus said, "But is not their beauty wonderful to behold? Do you not feel good when you look at them?"

"Yes," he answered.

Jesus said, "I tell you this: You and your wife shall grow in your love too. You will bring beauty and happiness to others. The Father called your child home, but there are many here who need love."

We Are All Brothers and Sisters

Jesus was pleased on what had been for him a quiet, soul-searching day. He looked at the crystal-clear waters lying before him. The ripples glistened and shimmered in the hot, sparkling sun. Peter also seemed to be mesmerized by their beauty, for it looked as if the sky touched the waters. "How beautiful," Peter said to no one in particular. All who sat near Jesus seemed to be lost in thought or in prayer.

Then the sound of men arguing reached the ears of Jesus and his disciples. Peter shook his head and said, "I thought for just one day we could spend time with our own thoughts."

Jesus raised his hand to acknowledge the travelers. "Welcome," he said. "Soon we will have supper. Will you join us?"

"Oh, no," John sighed. "How, with as little bread as we have?"

The travelers said they were weary and thirsty but offered to share their food too. "Let us eat first, and then we shall talk."

"Fine," Jesus said.

One man said: "Master, I have come a long distance. I had to talk to you with these, my brothers. In our town there are many strange people. They do not believe as we do. They go around with their heads uncovered, they do not pray, they go to the fields and eat flowers and not much grain, and they sing—oh, do they sing—but no one can understand them. They wash their hands constantly. I do not understand, Master. I feel we should get rid of them, and yet there is no way to do that. We have tried to ignore them, and we do not buy from them."

A younger brother broke in, "Yes, I have even spit at them, Master."

Jesus said, "Is this the way to treat your brothers?"

"Oh, no, they are not related, Master. They are strange. They share the house next door to us, and we must put up with their . . . with their . . . "

"With their what?" Jesus asked.

The men looked at each other, and Jesus said, "My friends, remember, we all come from the Father. We are here to teach, and, yes, we are here to learn. We must learn from one another. We must watch, observe, and try to understand them. If we think they are doing something wrong, we must speak to them. But we must not cast them aside. We need to understand them. The Father has given us minds to use, and we must use them. He has also given us hands to use, and we must also use them."

And then he said: "We have supped together. You have shared your food with us, and we have shared our food with you. We must also share our thoughts and our goodness." He continued: "In the field there are many flowers. Not all are the same. There may be more of one kind than another, but that does not mean that it is a better flower.

Remember, they are your brothers. If their skin is different or their speech is different, they are still children of the Father."

This is not what the visitors wanted to hear. Jesus said, "You do not have to believe me now, but go home and think about it, and I shall ask the Father to shine his light into your minds like the sun."

Caring for Our Brothers and Sisters

A merchant slowly approached Jesus. In his hands he bore gifts of bread and oil for Jesus. He said: "I have come with humility to you, Master. I want to share what I have with you."

Jesus nodded and said, "My disciples and I appreciate the food you have brought to feed us."

The man sat down and said: "I have been a merchant for many years, and age is now upon me. I have heard about you and I have listened to those who speak your words, but I must ask you in all honesty how do they apply to me as I travel from place to place, selling my wares?"

Jesus looked at the man and answered, "One must be honest and truthful not only toward others but also to oneself."

The man looked down, nodded and said, "Fine, and what else?"

Jesus continued: "You go from place to place and meet many people. Along the road have you ever come across people who cried out for a crust of bread or a drink of water?"

The man nodded that he had.

Jesus asked, "And did you share anything with them?"

The merchant thought for a while before answering: "At times I have, Master. Sometimes I have thrown bread to them because I did not want to be too close to those who are unclean."

Jesus questioned him, "You threw the bread?"

The merchant answered, "I tell you I was not going to get close to those who are unclean."

Jesus replied, "But were they not your brothers?"

The merchant looked rather strangely at Jesus and answered, "I never saw them before in my life."

Jesus said: "We are all children of the Father. Would you want to be treated in such a manner? Could you not have placed the bread at the side of the road and offered a kind word to them?"

"Yes, I guess I could have. But again I ask you, what does your teaching have to do with me, a merchant?"

Jesus answered: "There is so much and yet so little that you have done. I know you are basically a kind man, but you are not always understanding. You must learn to be both."

Then Jesus looked down at the bread the man had given him and said, "First, I will share this with my disciples and those who are hungry. Then and only then will I partake of it."

Anger in the Crowd

The men stood around the square talking. And then, like a bolt of lightning, the noisy square suddenly became quiet as a man cried out: "Hey, you, Jesus of Nazareth, who is your Father?"

Jesus turned and said, "Who addresses me?"

The man answered: "It is I. You can see me, can you not?"

"Yes," replied Jesus, "and whose son are you?"

The men in the square began to laugh. Jesus raised his hand, and it became silent. "I am the Son of God, and I am also the son of Joseph the carpenter."

The man asked: "How can you be the son of both? One so low and the other so great?"

Jesus answered: "We are all children of the Father. But we have earthly parents who guide us. They are to protect, to love, to teach, and to nurture us so that we may grow."

The man began to laugh as the others did. But there was no expression on Jesus' face.

Then a young woman dared to speak, "Jesus of Nazareth."

He responded: "Speak, woman."

The men became angry and cried out that no woman had a right to speak in this place. "Be gone with you," they yelled.

"No," Jesus said, "she has as much right to be here as we have. Speak, woman, speak."

She spoke out clearly, "Jesus of Nazareth, son of the Father, I ask you, when our lives are over, will we know you?"

Jesus nodded. "You will not forget me," he said. "No one will ever forget me. You will try to destroy the words I have spoken, that were given to me by my Father. But I tell you this: Each person is responsible not only for himself or herself but also for his brothers and sisters. Have no fear, but we will all be judged, and no coin will influence the judge."

Then he turned and slowly walked away. Peter said: "He did it again. He made them angry."

How Should Jesus' Followers Live?

esus was pleased with the group of young men whose questions were well thought out and probing. One raised his hand nervously and asked: "Master, I know I have asked this question before, and you have answered it, but if I wanted to be a follower of yours, what should I do and how should I act? How should I live?"

The other men snickered. Jesus looked sternly at them and said, "It is an honest question." The snickering and laughter ceased.

Peter cleared his throat and wondered what the Master would say. Jesus looked at the young man and said: "You are already like me, for we all come from the Father, you and I as well as all who sit here. The Father has many sons and daughters. Each in his own way and time will respond as a son or daughter should to the Father. We become one with the Father, and we learn from one another. At times one is the teacher and at other times the student."

"To be like me is to have respect for all, to have a listening ear, a helping hand, and to understand that all people have problems. To be like me is to try to understand and help them find the right path. One must teach. It is good to work with the hands and with the mind. One must have respect for the young and want to teach them so they may not fall prey to evil." Then he looked down at his hands, raised them, palms up, and said: "Remember that the Father has given us the ability to work with others who do not understand our ways. To teach may be likened to taking gold and placing it in the hands of those who are less fortunate."

Then he went to the young man, placed his hand on his right shoulder, and said: "You must also comfort others, care for people, and follow the rules of the Father, incorporating them into the ways of the world so that it may become a better place for those who live with you now and those who will come after you. Daily prayer is very important. Pray that you may walk the right path."

Peter smiled and said, "Master, when the work is done, what should this young man do to be more like you?"

Jesus said pensively, "The work will not be done until the final curtain falls on this life."

Love Gives Comfort and Strength

Jesus sat, head in his hands. Peter placed his hand on Jesus' head to comfort him, and, old man that he was, said with great compassion, "My friend, I have always thought you to be untiring."

Jesus responded, "Peter, Peter, I am so tired, so weary."

"Master, many times I have seen you when you needed to rest, but I have never seen you this exhausted."

"Yes," said Jesus, "I want to keep going. One part of me says 'rest for a while,' but another part says 'share and heal and teach while there is still time.'"

After a pause Jesus continued, "I have questioned my Father: 'Why me? Why have you given me life upon the earth?' And then I think about my mother and how unselfish her love for me has been. She forced a smile to hide her tears when she bid me goodbye."

Peter gently patted Jesus' back. "Master," Peter said, "what can I say, what can I do to make you feel better?"

Jesus took a deep breath and said: "Peter, just by being here, by caring about me, and by loving me you have eased me. I know the burden is mine alone to carry, but by offering your love you have given me strength."

Peter remained with Jesus, for even the Master, the Son of God who was soon to give his life for all, needed comfort and love.

Important Lessons for Life

Obligations to the Heavenly Father

Jesus was happy to see his friend, a man of wisdom who was advanced in age, walking toward him along the road.

"Master, I have come to visit you," the old man said.

"Why did you not come when I was in your town not long ago?" Jesus asked.

"I was there, but you couldn't see me," he answered. Then he chuckled and said teasingly, "Master, would it be fitting for me to visit you in my own home?"

Jesus thought for a while and then asked: "Why then is it fitting for you to visit me in my home?"

The old man smiled and remarked, "You are a cunning and wise man."

"Cunning, no," Jesus answered. "Wise, yes, but only in the ways my Father has given me."

The old man said, "I came when I was sure no one else would be around, because I was afraid what I wanted to ask might seem foolish to others."

"A question is foolish only when the person who asks it thinks it is," Jesus said.

"Well then," the old man said, "it will soon be time to observe Passover, right?"

"Yes," Jesus answered.

"Will you observe it?" the old man asked.

Jesus nodded and said, "Yes, why do you ask?"

"Why?" the man repeated with feigned astonishment. "If you are the Son of God, why should you observe it?"

Jesus sighed and sadness filled his eyes as he looked at the old man whose darkened skin was covered with sweat. "Everyone has obligations to my Father, for without his love, none of us would be here. If one man feeds another, should he not thank him? If a woman cries out 'I cannot see,' will not someone guide her? If a parent cries out 'my son is dying; save him,' does not my Father either heal him or give that parent strength to bear the sorrow? Should we not thank the Father for the life he has allowed us to bring into the world and for taking our loved ones home again to be with him? The prayers we use were handed on to us by our father's father and the fathers before him."

Jesus continued, "I tell you this: If you do not love my Father, why then do you preach his word?

The wise old man thought and then answered, "Because my father and his father were guides to our people."

"I am a guide too," Jesus said. "I do not wear the same robes you do, but I often speak the same words. We do not always agree, for there will be disagreement over my Father's rules, but I respect you. Like children we love our Father, each in our own way. I tell you this: No one can deny my Father's love because he and he alone gives life."

The Gift of Memory

*J*esus looked around at his disciples. His heart felt like it was bleeding when he saw how lonely they were because they had not seen their families for such a long time. He said to them: "We have spent much time here in prayer and fasting, and I have taught you all I know, but I can see the sorrow in your hearts from missing your family and friends. Even though we have one another, we long for those who are not with us."

A young man said to Jesus: "Master, I have truly enjoyed this time with you and I shall never forget you, but I can't wait to see my parents. Just thinking about them brings tears to my eyes."

Another disciple said, "Master, I too am grateful for the time I had to spend with you, but I long to see my child, to hold her, and to love her."

Before Jesus could answer either of them, still another said: "Master, I miss my wife so much. She died. I remember the times I was good to her and the times I was not so good. Many times she cried out in pain, but I pretended not to hear because I was tired and weary."

Still another spoke up: "Master, when my son died, I held his lifeless form in my arms. Oh, how much I wanted him to live, but now all I have is memories. I have had such a hard time putting them out of my mind while I've been with you."

Jesus half-smiled and said: "My friends, when we are alone, our mind works harder. We see things as we have never seen them before, we feel things more deeply, feelings arise more easily, and we long to hold those we love. Emotions are an important part of us. Animals too feel pain; they too are concerned about their offspring and care for them. But the bonds among them are not as strong as the bonds among us, for we have been created in the image of the Father. So you can imagine the sorrow the Father feels when we say no to him and the joy that fills his heart when we follow his rules."

Sharing What We Have

*A*n old woman, her head hung low and her body bent and tired, walked with great difficulty toward Jesus. He went to her, placed his arms around her deformed shoulders, and said, "Mother, come and sit with me."

She looked up at him and said, "I am not your mother."

"But aren't you *a* mother?" Jesus asked.

"Yes," she said, "but only in name now, for two of my sons were cruelly put to death. Their blood flowed from their bodies until there was no more. Another child was born deformed. My father and husband took this child from me, and I never saw him again. I was told they didn't feed him. My mother was covered with sores and lived among those who were unclean. Master, Master, my own body aches with pain. I have seen so much suffering. Why, Master, why?"

Jesus thought for a while and then said, "Woman, what you have experienced and felt has touched your heart, has it not?"

"Yes, Master."

"And have you not always been helpful and cared for those about to give birth?"

"Yes, Master."

"And have you not left bread for those who are unclean?"

"Yes, Master. Many times I have been hungry, but I always share what I have."

"Why?" Jesus asked.

"Because I know what it is like to suffer. I heard my mother cry when no one would give her a crust of bread; and I held my sons in my arms while they bled to death from their wounds."

"Woman, I tell you this: Even though your tongue has been sharp at times and you have cried out 'why me,' you have given comfort and love to those in need of it." She began to weep as he continued. "Not only have you shared your sorrow with others, but you have also cared for them. In so doing, you showed them that they are not alone; you have lessened their burden. You are working in behalf of my Father and me. I tell you this: Many will see things they do not care to see, and some will hide their eyes in fear, in shame, or in disbelief. But they must not do this. They must speak out, condemning those who have committed atrocities, for those who do not are as bad as those who have done the work of the evil one."

Helping Others

Jesus sat staring at the rough, choppy waters. Suddenly John said to him: "Master, look over there. A man is struggling in the water, trying to drag his boat to shore."

Jesus neither said nor did anything.

Then Luke said, "Let's go help him."

Still Jesus neither spoke nor moved a muscle. They couldn't believe he would just sit there and watch.

The fisherman continued to struggle, holding on to his boat by a rope and swearing loudly the whole time, as inch by inch he was slowly being dragged out to sea. He yelled for help, and only then did Jesus say, "Come, we must help our brother." They looked at him with surprise but said nothing and ran with him into the cold, angry waters.

Even with seven of them pulling together, the task was not easy. Their hot sweat and the cold waters alternately bit at their eyes and the skin on their faces, but eventually they dragged the boat to shore where they collapsed in exhaustion. The fisherman wiped the sweat from his forehead and said: "This is my only livelihood. I knew I shouldn't go out alone, but I prayed to God for protection before I set out. Just look how he listened to me! He nearly destroyed my boat and me along with it."

Jesus just stared and said nothing until the man began to curse both the waters and the heavenly Father. Jesus looked at his disciples, who were silently thanking God for his help, and at the angry, ungrateful fisherman. Then he looked up and said: "Father, forgive him. He doesn't understand."

"Don't understand what?" the fisherman asked defiantly. "All I know is that if I had depended on your Father, me and my boat would be on the bottom of the sea now."

Jesus said, "When you called, we came."

"But why didn't you come as soon as you saw me struggling?"

"Why didn't you call sooner? Were you afraid or too proud to ask for help?"

Peter said, "Master, I would have gone to help, but you said nothing."

Jesus said, "Many people do not help until asked or told to do so. Both ways are wrong." He addressed the fisherman: "My Father's love is always there when you call on him, but now that you are safe on the shore, you only curse him and shout defiance. And you do not thank these, your brothers, who have helped you."

"They are not my brothers," the fisherman said angrily.

"All men are your brothers," Jesus said. "I tell you this: If we had not all pulled together, you would not be here now to curse my Father. When we care for one another and share with one another, love binds us together into a family. We must not shut our eyes, our mind, our ears, or our heart to others' suffering. We must not be the last to come, but the first. For no one walks alone. My Father walks with all."

Not by Bread Alone

*T*was a very hot day, and those listening to Jesus teach were wiping their brows continually, but Jesus continued. The heat didn't seem to bother him.

Judas was concerned that some of the rich people might leave because of the heat, and so he invited them to sit under a tree, saying: "There will be shade, and it won't be as hot. I'll give you some water to drink."

He was leading them off to the side when Jesus said, "Judas, bring the water here so that all may drink."

Judas was upset, but he brought it to Jesus, who gave it first to a poor beggar. Judas was annoyed because he knew the beggar didn't have a coin to give them.

After Jesus had finished teaching and everyone had gone, Judas asked him: "Master, why did you give water first to the beggar? He couldn't give us anything, and the rich would have paid us well."

Jesus said, "Judas, Judas, is the coin so important?"

"But Master, we must buy bread."

"Judas, we do not live by bread alone. My words, my Father's words, are important to everyone—rich and poor alike."

Later Judas could be heard grumbling and muttering under his breath. Jesus called him over and asked, "Have I upset you?"

Judas said: "Again, Master, I must ask you: Why didn't you give the water to the rich first?"

Jesus answered: "I told you before. All men are welcome to hear the words of my Father. Both rich and poor shall sit at his table. There will be no division."

Judas said: "But this is the earthly world, Master. We must give the rich a special place so that they will help the poor."

The Master said: "Like you, Judas, some people bow before the rich, but others turn their backs on them and curse the day they were born. Those who have used their gifts and gained riches are blessed when they give to the less fortunate. When they give to them, they give also to my Father. But, on the other hand, those who become poor because they haven't helped themselves have wronged my Father. Many times the rich must teach the poor who have tried to help themselves without success, so that they can feed and clothe themselves and not be dependent on others. We must help one another, but if the poor become lazy and don't try to help themselves, then even the rich must turn their back."

Judas didn't like Jesus' answer and said, "Without the coin, Master, you couldn't teach, for you would be too hungry and weak."

Jesus said: "We must not think only about bread that sustains the body. We must seek spiritual bread—the words of my Father. You wanted to give water to the rich because you wished to receive something in return. Rather, give freely, and My Father will return your gift."

Judas still didn't understand. His mind was unbalanced by his hunger for coin.

A Lesson from a Drop of Water

*J*esus watched intently while drops of water slowly formed on the edge of a rock and dropped quietly onto a rock below. He could see what was happening but could not hear anything.

A wise old man sat down near Jesus and asked, "Why are you staring?"

Jesus smiled and said, "Perhaps I am waiting to hear what sound the drop of water makes when it falls upon the rock."

"Why?" the man asked.

"Why?" Jesus responded. "Perhaps I am waiting, as my Father waits, for people to call out to him saying 'I love you,' 'I need you,' 'be with me,' 'walk with me,' 'hold me when I am filled with sorrow,' 'wipe away my tears' 'comfort me.' 'Tell me that it will be a new beginning when the sun rises tomorrow,' 'assure me that the wheat will grow,' 'tell me that there will be no more sickness or hunger,' 'and promise that one day people will live in harmony.'"

Then Jesus reached out, caught a drop of water on his finger, and extended it to the wise old man.

The man just smiled and said, "One drop, what can one drop do?"

Jesus answered: "It is like a tear, and one tear can bring many more. One tear shed because a person realizes how his or her sins have hurt the Father, one tear of love, one tear shed for the harm done to a neighbor—these can do much good. There is hope even in this one drop of water because it can give comfort to a man dying from thirst."

The wise old man looked at Jesus and said, "You seem to be saying there is life in a drop of water, and that we are like drops of water."

"In many ways that is true," Jesus said. "And all of us together make an ocean." Then he sighed and said: "I could not hear the drops of water as they fell upon the rock. If I could have, it may have given me comfort. But the rock is hard, as are many hearts when tears fall upon them. There is much pain in this world. My Father's heart is not made of rock, and his love is like this drop of water. Even though you may not hear it when it falls upon you, it leaves its mark."

Taking One's Life

$\mathcal{T}$was one of those long, hot summer days. Jesus tried to find relief from the heat by sitting in the shade of a tree. He was hot but content, as were those who had just listened to him teach. A woman who had stood at the back of the crowd came forward now. She was troubled, and her voice quivered as she tried to speak.

"Master," she said, shaking, "my son, my only son, has taken his own life."

Jesus extended his hand to her and said, "Come and sit with me."

She sat down and said: "Master, did I do something wrong? Did I say something wrong? Is it my fault he killed himself? Didn't I give him what he wanted? Or did he just want to return to the Father?"

Jesus took a deep breath and said: "Woman, woman, I cannot speak for your son or for anyone else who commits suicide. No one knows what goes on in such a person's mind, and even less what is happening in the heart. But I can tell you that only a troubled mind would do this, a mind that does not think clearly. I would compare it to what happens to clear water when a handful of earth is thrown into it; it becomes cloudy. A cloudy mind does not realize that life is a precious gift."

He continued: "We are not all perfect when we come to earth. Many of us must work through difficult problems while we are here. Some are born crippled, blind, or diseased. But much is to be learned by these people and by those around them. Woman, do not break your heart. Ask my Father to be understanding when your son reaches his door, for I know my Father is loving and merciful. He will not blind your son with the darkness of the evil one. He will show him why what he has done was wrong—a sin. Fear not, for there is much love in my Father's heart. Now go, woman, and comfort another who is troubled like you. Do not condemn yourself or your child. Only my Father is his judge. No one else."

A Man Filled with Bitterness

The sun was peeking through the cloudy sky. Another long day, Jesus thought as he spoke to a group of men. As he spoke, one man in the crowd shook his head and smirked. A snicker formed on his lips. Jesus said nothing but continued to speak. All at once thunder clapped, and the men sought shelter.

But the man who was silently showing great disrespect came near Jesus, looked him in the eye, spat on the ground, and said: "You, a son of a carpenter, a teacher? Yes, you speak about caring and sharing, and you sound like you have great wisdom, but where does it come from? I see how these men hang onto each and every word you speak. But who do you think you are? You are no better than I or any of us. In fact, I believe I have more coins in my pocket than you, a son of a carpenter." And again he spat upon the ground.

Jesus said nothing but let the man go on and on and on. And then he said, "Be silent." The man was shocked. Rain was now slowly falling from the heavens. Jesus said: "You have spoken your mind, and now it is my turn. Can you tell me why you feel such anger?"

"I already told you," the man answered.

Jesus shook his head and said: "My friend, my friend, the anger is within you. Are you afraid of the words I speak because I am firm in my belief, because I am unbending? These are the Father's rules, not mine. I am only an instrument, an instrument to guide you on your path. But if you do not wish to follow that path, then I can only say I am sorry. Do you want to seek out another who will bend the truth when you wish? I tell you this, my friend: We are all children of the Father. He loves me no more than he loves you. I am not saying it is wrong for you to disagree with me, but bitterness and hatred in you make you not to want to listen. If you have something to say, then speak it with justice, not with hatred."

The man slowly lowered his eyes to the now rain-soaked, muddy earth. Jesus put his hand on the man's shoulder and said: "My friend, cast the bitterness away. Let your mind not be clouded like this muddy earth, but look," and he pointed to the sky, "and see the light. It is still shining. Let the light touch your mind and your soul and be healed of the pain you wish to inflict on others by accusing, degrading, and hurting them."

Jesus Is Moved to Tears

*J*esus walked slowly from the city. Everyone could see that tears had reddened his eyes and left marks on his cheeks. It was Peter, as usual, who had the courage to ask, "Master, why do you weep?"

Jesus wiped away the tears with his hand, leaving a smudge mark on his cheek, and said: "I could not stand what I saw. It was very disturbing."

"Master, are you referring to that young girl?" Peter asked.

"Yes," Jesus answered, "watching so young a girl sell herself for a coin breaks my heart. And yet, I know it is her way of providing bread for her family."

Jesus looked down and said: "Many people in the city claim they cannot help her, but they have safely hidden many coins."

"Maybe they don't know about her family's needs," John said.

"They know," Jesus answered with strong conviction; "I tell you this, however: I blame most of all those who have taken advantage of this child in her need. They have placed her in a position that harms not only her body but her mind and soul as well. For she will grow as hard as a rock. She will no longer be able to cry other than bitter tears that will sting her. I tell you this: Those who do not try to help her will feel the wrath of my Father."

John turned and said, "Then tell me, Master, why doesn't the Father change the world so that no one has to go hungry?"

Jesus looked at him and said: "John, my Father is not responsible for this. It is the result of the sins of those who have gone before us. We must struggle to restore the goodness that has been lost."

The Pain We Inflict on One Another

*J*esus sat quietly while a young man spoke. There was no emotion on the young man's face, but his hands grasped the cloth of his cloak and twisted it.

Peter said to John, "Why can't people see what harm violence does?"

John hushed Peter and replied, "Let's listen to what the Master has to say."

But Jesus continued listening, showing no emotion, until the young man had finished speaking. Then Jesus extended his hand to the young man, sighed, and said, "We do not understand the pain and suffering that we can inflict on others."

Jesus picked up a twig, which snapped loudly when he broke it. He broke it a second time and a third time. Then with his sandal he crushed it into the ground. Only the mark of his sandal and a part of the shredded twig could be seen.

He said, "After a person uses violence the first time, it continues like a chain over and over again. The person becomes enmeshed in either fear or excitement and asks, 'Is this what I should do? I have to be the stronger one. I will be the one to inflict pain.' Perhaps such a one hides in fear of others who might prove stronger."

Then Jesus bent down once again and picked a beautiful wildflower growing near a rock. He pulled off its petals one by one and said: "This is what violence does to the young. It destroys the beauty and the gifts given to them by the Father."

Jesus extended his hands to the young man and said: "Sin no more. Do not raise your hand in anger to another or use words that sting and hurt. Remember the twig and the flower. I tell you this: What you do to another you do to the Father. All of us are creatures of God. Do not use words or actions that do harm to others and destroy parts of their lives. Remember, payment must be made not to those whom you have hurt but to the Father."

Disagreement and Anger

As the disciples sat around a fire discussing what had happened that day, Peter said, "Master, if we are all God's children, as you have told us many times, if it makes no difference what the color of our skin is or what language we speak, if the Father still loves us even when we are physically handicapped or blind, if we are all brothers and sisters, then why can't we be civil to one another? Why is anger often in people's words and actions toward one another?"

John said impatiently: "Peter, it has been a long day for Jesus. Have you been thinking about that question for months?"

"Maybe years?" another added.

Jesus smiled and said: "Peter, Peter, it is a good question, an appropriate one. You are right. Even among you at times there is disagreement. Think of the words you exchanged with one another just seconds ago."

He continued: "Why don't people agree with one another? Perhaps it is a consequence of what happened at the beginning of life. We see in another something we want, and we become envious. Or perhaps something has been taken from us, and so we have a disagreement. Life does not always seem to be the wonderful gift it is. Even though life can be marked by struggle, it is a time for learning, growing, and sharing in many ways."

Jesus reached down, touched a flower struggling for life near a rock, and said, "Look. There is little soil for its roots, and so it fights to survive. In many ways life is like this flower; it too is often a struggle for survival. But life remains a beautiful gift. To learn its mysteries, you must learn to appreciate and enjoy its gifts—the freshness of the water, the warmth of the sun, the rain that falls and gives life to the soil, the life that grows within a woman, the scholar's hunger for knowledge, a child's first step and word, and the knowledge that there will no longer be pain or suffering in the presence of the Father after death. The experience of love is both a form of learning and a source of joy. So, again, why do people disagree with one another? It can be a way of learning more about one another and maturing. I tell you this, my brothers: There will be disagreement until the end of time, but we must learn to overcome it and live together in harmony. We need to be like this flower, which struggles to live and will not give up. This rock may be unmovable by now, but in the future humans will be able to lift it easily so that the flower can bloom and multiply."

A Lesson from a Beggar

*J*esus and his disciples slowly approached the house of Simeon the merchant. The sound of laughter and merriment and the smell of food from the house reached the weary travelers.

Judas said to Jesus, "I thought we were going to be the only guests."

Jesus remarked, "This is the house of Simeon, not the house of Judas."

The others smirked, and Judas looked down, embarrassed.

Jesus said: "I do not mean to be harsh, but Simeon lives here. He can invite whom he wants."

They began to slowly climb up to the house. When Simeon was told by his servant that his company was coming, he went out to greet Jesus and his disciples. "Welcome," he cried out, and then he embraced each and every one of them.

Jesus said to Simeon: "You have invited many people. It will be a great pleasure to meet your friends."

A shy smile, almost childlike, filled Simeon's face and he said, "I know you will be pleased by their presence, but your friends may not be."

When they entered the house, there were many people that Jesus' disciples recognized as those who begged at the gates of the city. Judas turned to Jesus and said: "I cannot believe my eyes. This man of great wealth invites beggars to eat with us."

Jesus turned to Judas and said, "Do you think you are any better than they?"

Peter hushed them both and said, "Be silent, or they will hear us."

Jesus nodded to each guest. As the bread was broken and the meal begun, Judas was appalled at what he saw, for there seemed to be no caring or respect for the host.

After the meal was finished, the beggars slowly left, some hobbling out with crutches and others dragging their legs behind them. Simeon said: "I know some of you are troubled by what you have seen. But when I was ill, I remembered your words, Master. Once when I reprimanded a beggar who came to you, pulling at you and asking for a coin, you said to me: 'You do not understand those who live a different life than you. Be understanding, be patient, and try to know and feel what they feel.' Later I broke my leg, Master, and I was laid up for many months. The pain and the inconvenience of not being able to walk were very difficult. I had to depend on others for the first time, and I realized what it was like to beg and to have to ask for help. And yes, Master, my life has changed. Many who begged at the gate are now employed by me. No, their quality of work is not always good, and at times it is very hard to be patient with them, but I have learned my lesson well."

Jesus nodded and said, "Simeon, it is not always easy to walk in another's sandals. You may see footprints and place your feet in them, but you cannot understand or feel the troubled mind or broken body of another until you experience it yourself."

Judas was listening to all that was being said. Jesus looked at Judas and reached out to clasp his hand. He said: "My friend, my friend, I know what troubles you, and yet I cannot speak about it, for it is not yet the time or the place. But remember, many will walk in your footsteps and do to me what you will do to me, yet many others will follow me and my ways."

Open Your Mind and Heart with Love

*J*esus watched and listened as three gentlemen sat and shared some bread with him. One said to him: "Master, we have told you what was on our mind. Now it's time for you to tell us what's on yours."

Jesus nodded in agreement and said: "It is good to share not only bread, which is the staff of life, but also what is in the mind and heart. Each of us has been given a gift, and when we share that gift we are truly blessed.

The second man said to Jesus: "Master, I have often thought about those who have lived before us, about the truths handed down to them, and the truths they have passed on to us. Will that chain ever be broken?"

"No, my friend, there will always be people who can teach and inspire others. A day will come when people will grow in knowledge and travel all over the world, touching every land and every body of water. Humankind will feel the clouds and understand more about the sun, the moon, and the stars. Just as we understand more clearly what was written a long time ago, so too those in the future will see the Father's gifts in a new light. As humanity spreads over the face of the earth, so too will knowledge of the Father increase."

The third man asked: "Master, do you think we understand the Father's words as well as those to whom they were first given?"

Jesus smiled and said: "Some do, but some never will. For unless people open their heart and mind with love, they will not understand the Father's words."

The Healing Power of Jesus

The Skeptic Who Wanted to Heal

A man came up to Jesus and asked, "Master, may I see your hand?" Jesus extended it, and the man began to study it closely, front and back, rubbing his coarse fingers over it, looking for something he couldn't seem to find.

"What do you see," Jesus asked.

"A man's hand" was the mocking reply.

"Then what do you wish to see," Jesus asked.

"Trickery," the man answered quickly. "I want to find out how you heal so many so that I can be like you."

Jesus sat down and sadly asked: "Why would anyone wish to carry a burden like this?" Then Jesus looked up into the heavens and said, although not loud enough for the man to hear, "Father, open my mind that I may guide him properly." Then Jesus invited the man to sit with him and said: "My Father has given the gift of healing to me that all may know his love. But they must open their mind and soul to receive this healing. Some are healed and their burdens are removed, but others must carry them throughout life."

"Why?" the skeptic wanted to know.

"I don't know," Jesus answered. "Only my Father knows. But I can tell you that it is the healer who carries the greater burden."

Again the skeptic asked why and assured Jesus that he still wanted this gift.

"You do," Jesus said, "but only for the glory and fame it would bring to you. My Father's gifts must never be used for one's own purposes but rather given away with love and caring. The healing power, like golden sunlight, flows through the hands and the soul into the hearts and minds of others in need. Those who heal are instruments of the Father, and one day they must stand in judgment before him and make an accounting of what they have received, how they have used it, and for what purposes. It will not go well with them if they have abused it. All honor and glory must be given to my Father."

The man got up and quickly began to back away.

"Be not afraid," Jesus said to him. "You will know if the healing power is within you. But do not ask for it unless you are willing to be abused and mocked in many ways."

"But why would they abuse a person who has healed them?" the man asked.

With a gentle smile and yet with sadness in his eyes, Jesus answered, "Because people are afraid of what they don't understand, because they fear what a healer may know about them, or because they don't know how to love or are afraid to return love. My heart is heavy and this gift hangs like a weight around my neck because I have come to share the Father's love and tell people about it. But in response, some honor only me and forget my Father, while others mock the gift he has given me and accuse me of trickery or of working with the evil one."

The man walked away, deep in thought. When he came to an olive tree, he made a fist and hit the tree trunk as hard as he could. Only the olives that were ripe fell. The man realized that only those who were ready to be healed could be healed. For it is God who does the healing, not the healer.

Jesus Desires to Heal the World

Jesus sat under an olive tree, energy spent. Both his body and mind were tired. He stared at his hands and said nothing.

John called, "Master, come and eat with us."

Peter added, "You are tired, Master, I know, tired of mind and body, but your body must have nourishment."

Judas snapped at the others: "Can't you see he is tired? We have been with the Master long enough to know that he does not need food as we do."

Peter's anger became quite apparent as his face reddened and he said, "Judas, you want more food for yourself."

And the two men began to argue.

Jesus raised his eyes then and said: "Be silent my friends. Can you not see that I am at prayer?"

"But you are looking at your hands," Judas said.

Jesus responded: "Yes, I look at these hands, for they have healed many people, and yet there were some I knew I could not heal. These are the ones I weep for."

"Why?" Judas asked. "You have told us your Father is good, that he loves us all, and that he will care for us. So why should you feel so bad? You have done your best, have you not?"

Again Peter got angry and said, "Do not talk to the Master that way."

Jesus said: "He has every right to speak to me like this. A person should speak what is in his or her heart and mind." He continued, "I wish I could heal the whole world."

Peter began to laugh and said: "Master, how could you do that? You are but one person."

Jesus replied, "In time, in time, you will carry my cross and you will heal."

"What cross?" Judas asked.

Jesus answered, "It will come." And slowly he walked over to the fire where the meal was laid out—bread and hot broth. Jesus slowly picked up the bread, broke it, and shared it with his followers. He said: "The power to heal is a gift that is given to some. At times one can heal his own body and at other times he cannot. Final healing must come from the Father in death. My friends, remember, one can always heal the mind with prayer, fasting, giving to another, listening, caring, and sharing." Then he looked down at the bread and said, "Let us eat, for there is much to be accomplished tomorrow."

The Healing Powers in Nature

A man was very angry and his words spewed forth as if from hot coals. Jesus listened patiently without uttering a sound. When the man's anger was spent, he sat down roughly and challenged: "Don't you have anything to say? I have told you about my troubles and expressed my anger. Have you no response? I have heard that you are wise, but I don't think so. You are just like that rock, silent and unmovable."

Jesus looked at the rock and said, "Yes, the rock has no voice, and it may be unmovable, but what, may I ask, are you sitting on? Is it not a rock? Does it not provide you with comfort? Is it not strong? And look, there is soil within its cracks from which new life has sprung forth."

The man looked at Jesus, then began to laugh, and said: "I came here in anger, but I guess I will return to my village with a smile on my face. You are indeed a wise man. In my village there are two who heal with herbs, soil, and ashes from the fire. I remember an old man who came through our village and said that nature has a gift for healing. I have heard that you heal as others do. Which is better, to heal with what grows in the ground or with the power found in a person?"

Jesus bent down and scooped up a handful of soil and said: "The Father has been good to all of us. He has given us the ability to use the power of the mind to heal. He has given us the ability to use what grows in the earth to bring comfort to people and cure them. We must learn to work with nature and nature will work with us."

Jesus picked up some of the moist soil near the rock and began to spread it over his hand. Then he sprinkled some water from a jar over it, making strange patterns, and said, "Life is like this."

The man looked at him and said, "I do not understand."

Jesus replied: "There are as many different roads to take in healing as there are roads to take in life. I tell you this: When we work with nature, we work with the Father, the Creator of us all. You came here and your words stung like hot coals, but you shall go back as meek and as beautiful as the flower that grows near your feet."

What Form of Healing Is More Important?

*P*eter said to Jesus: "Master, I have followed you for a long time, and yet there are still many questions in my mind and in the minds of the others. Yes, you have been kind and patient in answering questions, but I must ask you which is more important, the healing of a diseased body or the healing of a troubled mind?"

Jesus seemed to Peter to think for a long time before he answered: "It depends on the person. To heal both the body and the mind is truly a gift. To be able to heal the world, to heal the earth, to heal your neighbor is a gift—a gift we truly do not understand.

"Faith is a gift. Faith has healing power. To have faith in the Creator, to hand him your troubles, your pain, and your suffering, and to give him your joys, your happiness, and your thanks bring forth healing from within and radiate to all those whom you touch.

"Peter, Peter, someday you will be remembered as a healer of hearts, souls, and minds. You shall be strong like this rock, and people's faith will not be shattered, for you will instill in them strength, understanding, compassion and inner peace."

Then Jesus looked down at the earth, scooped up a handful of dirt, and threw it into the air.

Peter was mystified and asked, "Master, why did you do that?"

Jesus smiled and then laughed softly: "Let my words be carried by the winds. Let them be remembered by all. Let the earth be healed once again because we are in troubled lands, in troubled times, in troubled waters."

Two Different Healers

A man said to Jesus: "Master, I too am a healer. You claim that healing comes from the Father, but I think it comes from knowing people and their needs and from experience."

Jesus nodded.

The man said: "Then you agree we are both healers, Master? Why then do you teach that healing comes from the Father? I think it comes from within."

Jesus answered: "My friend, was it not my Father who gave you life—a body and a soul—and a mind so that you could discover the mysteries of healing? You have used your talents well."

The man thought for a while and then said to Jesus, "Master, then the Father has given the gift of healing to you."

"Yes," Jesus said, "but like you, I am not always able to heal."

The man asked: "Master, I can use a mixture of herbs and water to cure one person, but when I use it for another with the same symptoms, it doesn't always work. Why is this?"

Jesus answered: "I do not always understand my Father's ways. For I too have laid my hands on people and asked my Father to cure them, but it did not happen. Sometimes I feel a person may not be ready to be healed, and at other times I am sure the Father in his great wisdom knows what he is doing. Perhaps he wants that person to join him in his kingdom where he will be loved and suffer no more. I tell you this, my friend: My Father has given many people like you the gift of knowledge so that you may seek out and recognize the secret healing powers he has placed in the earth, the sea, and the sky. The Father never abandons us to pain and suffering. He has provided us with land so that we may grow wheat, water to drink and to cleanse ourselves, trees to give us fruit and shelter. The Father is wise, just, and loving."

The man looked at Jesus and said: "Master, there's something else I don't understand. Is it the evil spirits from the god of darkness who enter the people's minds and make them do strange and unnatural things?"

Jesus sighed: "My friend, my friend, sickness of the mind is not always caused by the evil one. The evil one touches all of us, for no one is free from sin. But I can say that there are times when the evil one will make his home within someone and cause that person much pain."

The man reached under his cloak and pulled out some leaves, a stone, some earth, and a handful of ground herbs. "Master, this is what I use to heal. What do you use?"

Jesus smiled and said: "I use the power I receive from calling out to my Father in prayer. That is what I use."

The Breath of Life

*J*esus was sitting on a rock, the waves lapping at his feet. His feet were tired and dirty from having walked many miles, and the water was cold and refreshing. As the sun set, it seemed to touch the water in the distance. It was a beautiful sight—a man at peace with the earth, the sea, and the sky.

The peace was broken, however, when young boy ran toward Jesus, calling out: "Is it you, Master? Is it you?"

Jesus smiled because he loved children and answered: "It is I. Come here, my child, come here."

The young boy exclaimed, "It *is* you—the healer, the teacher, the friend of all."

"What is so unusual about that? Are we not all called to be healers, teachers, and friends to one another? This is the way it should be."

The young boy said to Jesus: "Master, will you come to my home? My brother is ill, and I know you can heal him."

Jesus looked down at him and said, "If it is my Father's will, he will be healed."

"He has done nothing wrong," the young boy added. "He is young, younger than I am."

Jesus smiled and explained: "My son, my son, do you not understand? He does not have this affliction because of anything he or your mother or father or anyone else has done. It has come upon him through no one's fault."

Jesus slowly got his still aching feet and began the walk to the young boy's home. When they entered the house, they could hear heavy breathing.

That's my brother," the young boy explained. "He can hardly breathe."

It was almost dark inside the house, and the smell was overpowering. Jesus bent down and touched the sick boy. Jesus asked for some bread and water. Then he wiped the boy's face and said: "Let the waters cleanse you. Let the bread of life heal you." Jesus gently kissed the boy's forehead and, placing his mouth, over the young boy's mouth breathed into him. The boy coughed deeply and began to regurgitate. When he finished, Jesus wiped his face again and said: "I do not want you to eat anything for two days. Drink only this water. After two days eat a small piece of bread. You must change your diet and you must walk for exercise. Follow these directions, and you will be healed." The young boy did as he was told, and he was healed.

Two years later, when Jesus hung upon the cross, a young boy knelt beneath his broken, bleeding body and said: "Master, if only I could give you the breath of life you gave to me, I would. But all I can give are my tears and my love."

Healing with Mud

*T*had been a long, hot, difficult day, and Jesus was glad when the crowd had finally dispersed. It was peaceful in the garden, and he was pleased when a friend gave him some cool water to drink and warm bread to eat. Jesus broke off a piece, looked at his friend, and said, "Thank you for being so kind and generous."

"Oh, no, Master," the man replied, "it is you we must thank."

Jesus looked around and said: "The Father has been generous to me. The fields are producing abundant grain. In accordance with the law, I have urged the poor to gather what is left in the fields after the harvest. And even after they are finished, there is still much to return to the earth."

The man rubbed his leg and said: "Master, my legs really ache. I guess old age is catching up with me."

Jesus poured some of the water on the ground and turned some of the dirt into mud. He scooped some up with his hand and rubbed it on the man's legs and said, "Let the sun bake it dry and your legs will begin to feel better."

"Master, why do you use water and earth to heal me when all you have to do is speak a single word?

Jesus said: "My Father has placed upon the earth those things that can comfort and even heal us at times. Miracles will continue after I am gone. Some of those miracles will be performed by men and women who understand the powers within the heart and mind. Accept what I have given to you as a gift."

The man listened intently, and he believed.

A few days later one of the man's servants approached him: "Master, I heard what Jesus told you, and I saw what he did. I did the same thing to my wife, and now her legs do not ache anymore."

The man smiled and commented, "No matter how old we are, there is always something new to learn."

Jesus Heals with a Song

The young boy cried out in great pain. His body was badly burnt and the smell from it was terrible. Peter could not control himself and began to vomit. He was terribly embarrassed.

Jesus said: "Do not worry, Peter. You are old. I understand."

Peter was disturbed at his remark. It bothered him whenever anyone kidded him about his age. He was touchy about that. He replied: "Master, I may be old, but that stink is horrible. Why do you come to places like this? I'm tired and hungry, but now I can't even eat."

Jesus looked sternly at Peter and said: "Be silent. The child is in pain, but he can still hear."

The young boy begged: "Heal me, Master, heal me. I can't stand the pain."

Jesus replied, "I wish I could, my son."

"You heal others," the boy said. "Why won't you heal me?"

There were tears in Jesus' eyes when he responded: "I can only give you comfort. As much as I want to heal you, it is my Father's will, not mine, that determines who will be healed."

The young boy said, "It hurts so much."

Jesus began to sing, and the young boy listened.

"Sing with me," Jesus urged.

The boy's mother angrily said: "We called you to come here. We even sent a few coins so that you would come quickly. You accepted the coins, but you have not healed our son."

Jesus said: "I tell you again, it is my Father's will that is done, not mine. Come, let us praise the Father and thank him. This family, which was once divided, is now united."

Despite her anger, the boy's mother knew that what he said was true.

Jesus began to sing again: "Come, my children. Come, my children. Let us sing with joy. The Father loves his children, and the Father loves his son."

By this time John had rejoined them. He was dismayed when he heard Jesus singing in such circumstances. Jesus said: "It has been a tiring day for you. Come and join in our singing." But John couldn't stand the stench. Jesus told him: "This boy is innocent, but remember the smell, and let it remind you of sin. And now let us sing and be happy."

"Happy about what?" John questioned.

The boy's mother spoke up and said: "See, even another one of your own disciples believes you are . . . "

But her son raised his hand, placed two fingers over his mother's lips, and said: "Mother, it is true. When I tried to sing, I forgot some of the pain." His mother began to weep.

The young boy said to Jesus: "It was not my fault that I was burned. But now I know what it's like both to feel good and to feel pain. If it is the will of the Father and I live, I shall be happy and sing. I shall play for those less fortunate than I am. I will teach them that there can be joy in pain and sorrow."

Music—A Gift to and from God

Peter said, "Listen, Master, do you hear it?"

"Hear what," John said to Peter. "Your ears are old and mine are young, but I don't hear anything."

Jesus raised his hand, turned slightly toward the left, and said, "Be quiet."

The disciples seemed hardly to breathe. The music was very soft but pure and sweet. It increased slowly in volume, touching their hearts and minds. Jesus sat down on the rocky path and placed his head in his hands, taking in the beauty of the sound. And then the music ended.

Peter quickly called out: "Who is it that plays this music? Who is it?"

All the disciples called out in different directions. But Jesus sat still.

A figure appeared out of the shadows—a young man, slightly bent. In his hands he held a reed instrument. Jesus looked up and said: "Welcome, my friend. Your music is very pleasing. It is truly a gift." Even in the dimness of the approaching night the young man seemed to be embarrassed by the praise Jesus had given to him.

Luke said: "Never have I heard such a beautiful sound. It touched me deeply."

Peter said, "It comforted me."

John said: "I could hardly believe my ears. Where did you learn to play such beautiful music?"

The young man looked not at those who questioned him but at Jesus and said, "I was sick for many years. This instrument was given to me by an old carpenter who came to help my father. He fashioned it and said, 'Try it. It will give you joy.' I refused to touch it for many months, but one day I picked it up and prayed, asking our Creator to give me the ability to make beautiful sounds. I promised that if he would heal me, I would play for those who were sad or ill. I have kept my promise."

But it is the strangest music I have ever heard, " Peter said.

The young man smiled and said to Peter, "My friend, it is mine—my gift to our Creator and to all he has created."

Jesus nodded his agreement. "Along with the gifts we receive from the earth come gifts from the heavens that provide for us in many ways. Go, my son, play for others so that they may be inspired to listen for the sound of the angels who cry in the night that there may be peace and comfort upon the earth."

Then Jesus got up slowly, placed his arm around the young man's shoulder, and said: "You have given us great pleasure, my son. Go in peace."

The young man turned and began to play as he walked away.

When they could no longer hear him, Jesus said to those still straining to hear just one more note, "May the gift of the spirit be with him—a gift of love and joy so that through his gift he may open the hearts and minds of others to the wisdom and love of the heavenly Father."

The Healing Power of Laughter

Jesus sat alone.

"What troubles him?" John asked.

Peter grumbled: "Do you think I'm the only one who understands the Master? Don't you have eyes to see for yourself?"

John said, "I believe you usually do understand what the Master is thinking."

Peter replied, "Believe me, if I knew, I wouldn't be reprimanded so often."

Jesus looked up with a smile on his face and said: "It seems the two of you are talking about me again. What troubles you?"

Peter replied, "You mean what troubles him. He was curious about you and asked me what was troubling you."

Jesus responded: "Do you think I have a problem? Do I ever have a problem?"

They all began to laugh, and Peter said, "Well, Master, do you remember last week when a woman came up to you and . . . "

Jesus interrupted, "Say no more, say no more."

Then Jesus continued: "It is good to smile and laugh, but not in mockery. Laughter is a gift from the Father." Peter and John looked at one another. Jesus said, "When you see a newborn child, it is difficult not to smile admiringly at its beauty and simplicity—at a beautiful gift so pure and untouched by the problems of the world. And when you see flowers in the field, you have to smile, knowing there was great planning before this gift was given to us."

"Planning?" John queried. "The seeds are carried by the winds and the birds."

Jesus replied, "My friend, can't you give credit to the Creator for planning that? Don't you think he thought about these things beforehand?"

John began to laugh. Peter said, "I think John has been in the sun too long." And then he began to laugh too.

Judas walked up to them and joined in the laughter.

Jesus said, "What a joy it is to see my disciples so happy."

John said: "I don't know why that happened. Something just made me start laughing. It wasn't anything you said, Master."

Peter added, "I heard you laugh and I started to laugh."

Judas said, "Well, I thought the sun had gotten to both of you, but I couldn't help laughing too."

Jesus said, "Have you ever thought, my friends, that laughter could be contagious?" They looked at one another. Jesus continued, "What great joy it must be for the Father to see his children filled with joy. We have so much for which to be thankful."

❧

The Compassion of Jesus

Jesus Comforts an Old Woman

It had been a long, tiring day. And Jesus was glad to be able to rest for a while. He sat down near a tombstone in a burial field. It was a very quiet and peaceful place. While he was lost in thought and prayer, an old woman walked by him without noticing him. She stopped a short distance away and began to weep at her son's grave.

Jesus waited a few moments and then slowly approached the old woman. She was startled when she saw him and cried out: "Who are you? What right do you have to come and disturb my mourning?"

Jesus responded, "Woman, I have come to comfort you."

"Comfort me?" she said with disbelief, now recognizing him. "You who raise the dead, you who heal, you who did not . . . " Her tears prevented her from saying more.

Jesus slowly raised his eyes and looked directly into her tear-filled eyes and said: "Woman, death must come to all of us. But first we experience life, learning, and growth before we return to our creator." He paused for a moment and then said: "I tell you this, woman: Your weeping and wailing may help you, but they will not help others. Those who share your sorrow and who comfort you will not weep and grieve with you forever. There is a time to share genuine tears, but sorrow must end, even though it may be very difficult."

Jesus looked at the ground and said, "It is very peaceful and beautiful here." He sighed and continued: "Woman, do not weep for the dead. Weep for those who still have the breath of life."

The old woman asked, "Master, should I pray for my son?"

A smile formed on his lips and he answered: "Pray? Yes. Pray that he is at peace with the Father, that he no longer sees how his sins have marked the earth. Pray that he has learned his lessons well." Jesus then extended his arms toward her and said: "Woman, woman, it is the living for whom we must care. My Father will care for those who have gone to join him."

A Second Healing

Jesus sat on the ground at the top of the hill, the outline of his body framed by the red glow of the setting sun. He was drawing line after line in the dirt with a stick. It was difficult to tell whether his mind was just wandering peacefully or if he was deep in prayer with his Father. Only he knew.

The young man approached him cautiously, not knowing if he should bother him, and asked softly: "Master, can we talk for a while?" When he didn't answer, the young man didn't know if it was because he didn't hear him or perhaps didn't want to, but he edged a little closer, repeated his words, and reached out and touched Jesus' hand.

Slowly Jesus turned his head and asked: "Have you not already been healed? What more do you want me to do for you?"

The young man sat down and said, "Master, you have healed me of one affliction, but another has come upon me." And he held out his injured hand.

Jesus sighed and asked: "What do you want from me? You are young and strong." He looked deep into the young man's eyes as if he were looking into his very soul.

"Why did you heal me, Master?" the young man asked him.

Jesus responded: "It was my Father who healed you through me. We are all here to heal one another."

The young man shook his head in disbelief and said: "But, Master, my father is wealthy. He had sent me to the finest physicians. None of them could heal me. It was only when you, the son of a carpenter, placed your hands on me that warmth flowed through my body and I was healed. I knew immediately that I was to take hold of this warmth and never let it go."

A beautiful smile filled the Master's face and he said: "You have learned well, my son. I tell you this: When my Father heals, he heals for a reason, and for those who are healed, their life is no longer their own. They have been given a new set of scrolls that read: 'Give back to me what I have given to you.' Tell all your friends and neighbors what I have done for you. Live each day in perfect harmony with my words and my Father's rules."

Then Jesus paused, looked at the young man, and said, "Which would you rather give to my Father—your heart or your soul?"

"I do not understand. What do you mean?"

Jesus said: "I was hesitant when I placed my hands on you to heal you. I wanted to heal you, but I didn't feel as much love as I should have had for you. My human feelings said 'Do not heal him, for he will not be grateful,' but I prayed to my Father and said 'Take this thought from my mind.' And when I felt the energy flowing through my body, I asked my Father to increase it because of my doubt."

The young man looked at the Master and said: "When I went back to my village, I didn't tell anyone what you had done for me; even though I got stronger day by day. Then one day I passed a beggar dying along side the road. When he cried out for water, I spit at him and told him to go ahead and die, for such a dirty and worthless person would make good fertilizer for the soil. But I hadn't walked more than ten steps when I became so thirsty that my mouth dried out and my tongue swelled. I reached for my water, but there was none there. When I looked back, the beggar held out a water jar to me and said, 'Come and drink.' I ran and began to drink. When I was filled, I looked around, and he was gone."

The Master said nothing. He just smiled.

The young man said to him: "Those who are healed have a greater obligation toward others, don't they, Master?"

He said: "Yes, again I say, you have learned your lesson well."

When the young man looked down, his gangrenous hand was healed. He began to cry and said, "Master, you have healed me a second time."

"Not I," he said, "but my Father. And he has healed your heart, your mind, and your soul as well. Now share his gift and heal others." The sun was down by now and it was dark, but Jesus continued to make marks in the soil with a stick as if he were counting the lashes or the drops of sweat and blood that would soon cover his body.

John Feels Guilt at Being Healed

John had been very quiet all day long. He wouldn't even look into Jesus' eyes. Every time Jesus spoke to him, he lowered his eyes. He did his duties but offered no comments or opinions as he did. When the sun had gone down and the stars were beginning to shine in the night, Jesus said, "John, come walk with me." John obeyed but still did not say anything. "Is something troubling you, my friend?" Jesus asked.

"Oh, no, Master," John answered. "Why do you ask?" But the tone in his voice was not normal. It seemed to be tinged with guilt. There was hesitation in it, and that was strange for a man who truly believed Jesus was the Son of God.

After they had walked a short distance, Jesus said: "Can you not speak to me? I know what is in your heart, John, but speak it out."

John began to cry, and as the tears flowed he said, "Master, forgive me."

"How can I forgive you if I know not what I should forgive?" Jesus asked.

John said: "Master, you know I was away for three days and nights. I stumbled and fell the first night and hurt my leg. I should have stopped and rested, but I kept walking. By the time I reached the city, there was so much pain in my leg that I could hardly put any weight on it. An old man named Joshua was at the gate. He saw me limping and mentioned a woman who he said could help me. Master, I did not know what to do. I only had enough coins to buy bread. I could not pay to see someone. But he told me she was a kind woman and would help me. He took me to her, Master, he took me to her. And Master, she *was* a kind woman—a woman who could hardly see. She placed her worn and wrinkled hands on my leg and began to pray. Then she bathed it and wrapped it with leaves soaked with spices and herbs, and once again she prayed. She told me to continue doing this, and she gave me some broth. Master, it was so good and warm. By the next day I could place my weight on my leg. It still hurt, but not at all as it did before. And by the time, and by the time, Master . . . "

" . . . that you reached here," Jesus helped him out, "it was healed."

"Yes," John answered. "But I was ashamed to tell you for fear . . . "

"For fear of what?" Jesus asked.

"I was afraid that you would be angry with me, Master," John answered.

"Angry?" Jesus responded, "Oh, my son."

"But was it wrong, was it wrong to seek healing from someone other than you, Master?" John asked.

Jesus looked at John, extended his arms, held John by the shoulders, and said: "Is it wrong to seek another's help? Of course not, John. Did she harm you in any way?"

"No," John answered. "She was kind and understanding. She even fed me."

"Did she ask you for any coins?"

"No," John responded. "I didn't pay her anything because she said there was no need to. She said if I had anything to give her, I could lay it on the table, but even if I didn't, she would still help me."

"She is a good woman," Jesus said. "There are many in the world like her, John." And then Jesus looked down at his hands and said: "These hands were made to heal, not only the body but also the mind and the soul. And you, my son, have learned what one person can do for another. Pray, John, for we all have the ability to heal in one manner or another."

A Heart Filled with Sadness

A man said to Jesus: "Master my heart is filled with sadness. Two years ago my cousin, who was my closest relation and also my friend, was executed for stealing. He didn't steal for himself but for his family. My heart is filled with sadness because his family is still hungry and overcome with great sorrow, and I have lost a cousin and a friend. There are times now when I fear death. I wake up in a heavy sweat, crying out at the top of my voice. I hear that you are a wise man, and so I have come to ask you if you are afraid of death. Why should man die at the hands of others? Why can't we live together in peace?"

Jesus extended his hands toward the man and said, "My friend, we are not like this rock, which will remain on this earth forever. We are born to live, to grow, to learn, to teach, and to die. My heart and my prayers go out to you and your cousin's family. I am not his judge. I only know what you have told me."

The man broke in again and repeated, "But are you afraid of death?"

Jesus replied: "I will tell you a story. When I was very young, my mother and I passed by a cross, and she began to weep. When I asked her why she was crying, she held me close to her breast and said:

'Son, I fear the cross. It causes so much agony and pain. My eyes do not even want to look upon it for fear that someday, somehow . . .'

She did not finish, but she was sad for the next two days. I know her compassion and sadness were for those hung upon the cross. Do I fear death? At times. I wonder what will happen later in my life, and yet I know I must be strong and accept whatever comes."

Then Jesus looked down at his hands and said: "The Father has given us hands to work with. Why didn't your cousin work with his hands to provide for his family?"

The man shook his head and answered: "I don't know what possessed him to steal, but why did they have to take his life for that? Do judges have no compassion in their heart?"

A tear slowly trickled from Jesus' eye as he said, "I too have wondered why one man does not treat another man with respect and kindness." Then he sighed, looked up to the heavens and tears began to flow profusely from his eyes. He looked at the man and said, "Come, stay with us and we shall pray for his soul."

God Doesn't Answer My Prayers

There was great love and compassion in Jesus' eyes as he looked down at the child whose body was badly deformed. Her uncle, who had brought her to Jesus, said, "Master, I have taken care of her since she was born, hoping and praying that she would be healed."

Jesus reached down, picked up a smooth stone, which he rubbed between his fingertips, and asked, "Why have you opened your heart to this child?"

"Master, I had a dream and in it was the face of a person I was told I was to love and care for. I was also told a man would come my way who would heal her. It was her face I saw, and I believe you are the one who can cure her."

Jesus smiled and placed his hands on the child's shoulders. "My little one," Jesus said. But she didn't look at him or speak to him. Again he said to her, "My little one, look at me."

"No," she said in a very soft and shy voice.

"Why not?" Jesus asked.

"Because no one has been able to heal me, and God does not answer my prayers."

Without lifting his hands from the girl's shoulders, Jesus said to the man: "You still have not answered my question. Why have you taken care of her?"

"Master," he replied, "shouldn't we open our heart to others? We are blessed in many ways when we give to others."

Jesus said: "This child did not come to you. You are not her uncle. She is not related to you. You sought her out. Is this not true?"

The man hid his face and said, "Master, how did you know this?"

Jesus said: "It was with compassion and love that you took her into your home when you knew she would be abandoned. The two of you have loved one another. And I tell you this: My Father will reward you greatly in his home, for he knows all."

Jesus looked at the child again, and this time she looked up into his eyes. He touched her right cheek and then her left with his hand, kissed her, and said: "Be healed, my little one. But it will happen slowly so that you may know and understand and feel the love of my Father. To be healed too quickly would not be fair to the man who has given you so much love."

The child smiled and looked deeply into her "uncle's" eyes, which filled suddenly with tears. He said: "You have never looked at me like this before."

"I thought you were my father and that you were afraid to admit it. But now I shall call you Father joyfully, for you cared for me and loved me when my family abandoned me."

Jesus said, "My Father's heart and home will always be open to those who open their heart and home to a stranger in need."

A Visit to a Dying Friend

Jesus called into the house from the doorway: "It is I. May I come in?"

A man whose body was burdened by age and whose eyes were clouded called out from his bed, "Come, come."

His wife could not believe it when she saw that it was the Master. "Welcome," she said. "It has been a long time since my tired eyes have caught sight of you. Come."

Jesus smiled and placed his arms around her slightly bent shoulders.

"He is failing, Master," she said. "He is failing."

Jesus sat down next to the old man, placed his hand on his, and said, "I have come to visit you, to spend some time with you."

"You are so kind," the old man said. "Only a few think of me or come to visit me anymore." Tears began to form in his eyes.

"Do not think that," Jesus said. "Not coming does not mean that they do not think about you."

"Oh, Master," the old man said, "many, many people used to stop on their way through town and eat with us. Now I'm too tired even to get out of bed. I want to return to the Father's home."

"It is not your time," Jesus said.

He held the old man's hand, a hand that had often helped to comfort the sick.

The old man said: "Master, I can't do good for anyone. I can't even take care of myself. My wife has to care for me as a mother cares for a child."

Jesus looked at the man's wife and said, "I do not hear any complaints from her."

"No," she said, "I'm glad to have him, for he is always a source of comfort to me. We have many precious memories to talk about because many people have touched our lives."

"You have been a good man," Jesus said. "You have always comforted the sick. I can remember when I was a child and you came to visit my mother when she was sick. You spent some time with us and comforted my father. You were a good rabbi, a caring person, with great love in your heart."

The old man shook his head and said, "But no more do many people visit the sick."

A woman appeared suddenly at the door and called out with laughter, "I've got something for you."

She didn't recognize Jesus because his back was toward her. The old woman got up quickly and extended her arms to the young woman, who fell down on her knees and bowed when she realized it was the Master.

Jesus said, "Woman, it is I who should bow before you for you have come to visit the sick and you have brought a gift with you."

When she lifted her head, there were tears in her eyes. Jesus bent down, kissed her cheek and said, "You are truly blessed in my Father's home; when your time comes, he will not abandon you."

The old man said, "Master, she visits me, comforts me, and gives me help."

"This is the way it should be," Jesus said, "but many people have become concerned only about what happens in their own little world. They forget how much my Father wants us to spend a few moments with him and with those who need to be comforted."

Jesus then said to the young woman: "You are blessed and loved. Never forget that my love will be with you for all eternity.

A Woman Offers Her Pain to God

A young man came to visit Jesus, who was pleased to see him because he knew the young man's mother well. He said to Jesus, "Master, I beg you to come with me to visit a friend who is old and in great pain."

His request was difficult to grant because Jesus already had other plans. Many people were waiting to listen to him teach and to speak with him.

However, the young man was very sincere in his concern for this woman. He said: "She has been like a mother to me, like my very own mother, and so I cannot abandon her in her time of need. I even go to the well to get water for her." As he said this, he put his head down in embarrassment because that was woman's work and not man's work. Jesus understood, because he knew the humiliation that young men often suffered from women at the well.

Jesus said to Peter, "I will be gone for a while."

Peter became angry and responded, "But Master, you know people are already on their way here to see you, and there are many places we have to visit ourselves."

Jesus raised his hand and said, "Peter, Peter, be patient with me."

Peter cast his eyes to the ground and said with a sigh, "You are the Master and I am but a servant."

Jesus smiled, went to his friend, placed his arms around him, and said, "Peter, you do not serve me; you serve the Father."

Jesus went with the young man. Time seemed to stand still as they walked silently along the road. When they reached the woman's home, they could hear someone crying softly inside. Jesus entered and placed his hand on the shrunken, crippled form on the bed. As his eyes grew accustomed to the darkness, he saw a woman who was blind and who had terrible running sores all over her body. Her eyes were filled with tears of pain.

Jesus said to her, "Woman, woman, I want so much to heal you, but I cannot."

She responded: "I have not asked you to remove my suffering. I want to offer it to the Father for those who have sinned against him."

Jesus' tears fell upon her, and he said: "Woman, woman, you give me strength. I shall never forget your words—never."

As he turned to leave, a weak voice called out from the bed: "Be strong, my friend, be strong. Remember, the Father loves us."

Jesus smiled and said, "I know, old woman, I know."

⋑

Many Can Heal

Jesus sat among the crowd. He knew they were angry and that this was not going to be a good day, but he welcomed the challenge. And then, like a sudden rainstorm, they began to ask questions.

A man said: "Jesus of Nazareth, son of a carpenter, why should we listen to you? Some say you heal, but others say you are a fake."

Before Jesus could answer, another man rose and asked, "Jesus of Nazareth, how can we believe anything you say, for you are not a schooled man?"

The questions continued: "Jesus of Nazareth, you claim to have power to heal. I have seen you heal some people, but I have also seen some you could not heal. You excused your failure by saying it was not the time, that it was in your Father's hands. If you are his son, why do you not have as much power as he does?"

Then an older man was helped to his feet by his two sons. His eyes were dimmed by age, and his voice was almost inaudible. He said: "Master, why should we have faith in you? Why should we believe we come from a higher power? Most of us are poor, although there are among us some rich merchants. There are people here from many tribes—some you healed and others you did not—so I know you rely on faith. But you are not the only one who can heal." He motioned for his sons to help him sit down again.

Jesus raised his hand and said: "I will try to answer your questions. I know they were on your mind and you had to speak them out. It is right that you did so. But there is clearly anger and frustration in your voices and in your hearts. But I tell you this: I have enough faith to know I am loved by the Father, that I have a mission, and that it will be accomplished. To some I seem a failure. You—yes, you—have told me that I have healed some and not others. But it was not my decision. It was the will of the Father. As a dutiful son, I have obeyed."

He continued, "Oh, you of little faith. To lack faith is to be large like a mountain but have no strength. Look around you and ask for wisdom. Look at what the Father has given you, and base your faith on the knowledge that you must be loved for him to have created such beauty."

"But there are many who are hungry among us," another said.

"This is true," Jesus said, "but there still are fields to grow seed in and people who will feed the hungry. That is practicing faith, too."

Then he said: "When you feel you have been abandoned, look at the sun and the stars. Touch the earth and let the water flow through your fingertips. Look at those less fortunate and those more fortunate than you, and deepen your faith knowing that, like a field of flowers, my Father has many special gifts of love to share with you now and when you return to him. Even those who are poor, deaf, or blind have received gifts from the Father."

The Physician —
Healer of Heart and Mind

A young man dressed in fine robes came up to Jesus. Peter said to John: "Here is a man of great wealth. Do you notice how well he carries himself?"

John nodded in agreement.

When he approached Jesus the young man held out many coins to him. Jesus did not touch them but said: "These will be used for the poor, the hungry, and the sick. Give them to Judas, and he will care for them."

The young man seemed to be impressed by Jesus but said nothing for a long time while looking straight at him. Finally he said: "I am a physician, and I am well respected in my community. Yet, Master, I seek your wisdom." Jesus said nothing, and so the young man continued, "I heal people, but I feel there is a part of me that is not in tune with the whole bodies of those I heal."

Jesus nodded and said: "I tell you, my friend, you are generous. You care even for those who do not have any coins to pay you. There is kindness and understanding in your heart, but you as a physician must learn to heal not only the body but also the heart and the mind."

The young man nodded in agreement with Jesus and said: "But, Master, that is asking so much of me and my family. It demands that I spend much time away from them."

Jesus replied: "A physician is like those who preach the word of the Father. They must learn to deal with the whole person, to be an instrument to relieve their patients not only of their physical illness but also of all that weighs heavy upon their heart and mind. You must listen with both ears. You must see with both eyes. You must feel with your heart and your hands in order to draw forth illness from both the heart and the body."

Then Jesus looked down at the young man's hands and blessed them. Jesus said: "Now go, my friend, and you shall be a healer of both mind and body. Your love for those who are unfortunate shall bring them comfort. I thank you for what you have given to the poor because you know in your heart that the importance of coin is only that it can be used for caring and love. Your hands are blessed. Now go in peace, and my prayers and the prayers of others shall always be with you."

Love of Nature

Jesus, Joseph, and Nature

Jesus stood with his father and a very old man from the temple looking at the clouds. Typical of a young boy pursuing wisdom, Jesus said, "Father, what are you looking for?"

Joseph began to answer, but the wise old man spoke first, "My son, we see the Father."

"Where?" Jesus asked, "in the sky, in the clouds?"

Joseph smiled and nodding to the old man said: "My son, there is so much to learn in nature, so much. The Father is within each of us as well as all around us. He is in this piece of wood I have carved, in this rock, and in the sky."

Jesus sat down, thought for a while, and then said, "If he is everywhere, he must know all of us."

"Yes," the wise old man responded. "He knows even the smallest child."

Jesus looked up at his father and then at the old man and said, "You are trying to teach me, are you not?"

The old man smiled and Jesus then said, "If I am to be a carpenter's son, why must I know that the Father is in all things—in the wood, in the stone, in the clouds, and in me?"

Joseph answered, "My son, my son, if you have no one to teach you, how will you grow?"

"Like a tree," Jesus answered. "It does not need help from anyone."

"No, that's not right," the wise old man said. "A tree also needs help from the Father, for it needs the wind, the rain, the sun, and the night." Then he looked down at his hands, which had grown wrinkled from age, and said to Jesus, "The sun and time have done this." Then he looked up into the sky and said: "The light never grows tired of coming, the sun continues to shine, the trees give us fruit. We must continually praise the Father for all he has given us."

The Song of Nature

*J*esus stood in the rain with his disciples and said, "Listen."

They listened intently, and Peter finally said, "Master, I don't hear anything but the wind."

Jesus smiled and said: "Close your eyes, my friends, and listen to its song. It is a gift from my Father."

So they listened to the wind blowing—or was it singing?—through the trees.

"Listen," Jesus said, with excitement in his voice, "to the branches cracking in the wind, to the leaves touching one another, to the bird calling out to its mate, to the raindrops like tears from heaven falling upon the leaves, the earth, and the stones."

Jesus smiled, looked up at the sky, and let the rain wash his face clean. "It feels so good," he said, "for our journey was long and hot and dusty. The Father should be praised for providing us with great pleasure and great wealth in these drops of water, in the stones for our homes, in the trees that bear fruit, in the branches we use to build fires and bake bread, in the leaves that cover and shield us."

"They're not doing a very good job now," Peter complained, feeling more and more uncomfortable as the rain continued to fall.

"Nature is God's song, telling us of his love and revealing his secrets to us. Listen closely, my friends, to her voice. Learn all you can about the earth so that you will respect it. If you are good to it, it will be good to you and provide you with great abundance when you plant your seeds in its soil."

Judas said, "You speak as if nature is a woman."

"A woman and a mother," Jesus answered, "for she bears life each day, provides for our needs, and protects and loves us."

When Jesus bent down and picked up a twig, John said: "Oh, oh. He's going to teach us something. Every time he makes marks upon the earth, he gives us something to think about."

"But it's nothing but an old, dead twig," Peter said.

"Yes," John said, "but he makes it seem so valuable and so beautiful."

Jesus heard them but didn't say anything. Instead, he bent the twig until it made a loud crack and then said, "Each time I snap a twig,

I thank my Father for the gifts he has given us—and it speaks back to me."

Peter smiled and said: "Master, every time you break a twig, it's going to crack. There's nothing unusual about that."

"No, Peter," Jesus said, "it speaks. Have you not just listened to the wind and to the rain? Have you not heard how a thirsty person's voice changes when he or she has been given water to drink? Or how delighted a child is when cool water is poured over its body? Oh, my friend, the Father has given us gifts no person will ever be able to give us. We must thank him, for he has provided well for us and given us so much."

A Lesson from a Bird

The day was not warm. A cold breeze was blowing across the water. But Jesus did not notice it because the sadness and pain he felt were almost overpowering. Trying to console him, Peter said, "Master, I know your loss is great, but is he not with the Father as you have taught us?"

Jesus looked up at his friend and answered: "Yes, he is with the Father, and he is still with us. He was a man I respected and loved because he cared for me as if I were his son."

Then Jesus looked down at the earth, scooped up a handful of the sandy soil, and let it fall slowly through his fingers. He looked up at the clouds as the sky turned dark and said: "Father, Father, care for my friend as he cared for me. He will turn to dust, and we will not see him again here, but let his knowledge and love continue to flow through us and bear fruit. And let the seeds of truth he sowed bring us joy."

All of a sudden a bird landed close to Jesus' feet and began to sing a joyful song. A tear fell from Jesus' eyes as he bent down to caress its feathers. Surprisingly, the bird did not fly away. It seemed to be mesmerized by his loving gaze and his soft voice. Jesus picked up the bird very slowly and carefully, and then opened his hand wide and said, "Go, my friend."

Peter looked at Jesus very strangely and said, "Master, when you picked up the bird, you picked him up so gently, and then just as gently you told him to go."

Jesus responded: "In this life, we are born and then we die so that we may fly to a new place—to another world. The bird reminds us of the gift of nature that the Father has given to us. We show our love to him when we care for this gift. We must work with nature if we are to be one with the Father. We cannot survive without nature."

Stars Give Hope

Jesus and his friends sat around a fire to warm their weary bones. The hot broth they sipped was comforting. Jesus knew it was a good night for teaching and learning, and so he looked up into the sky and prayed for guidance so that his words would not be idle words but words from the Father that his followers would continue to teach when his time had ended and their time had begun.

Andrew asked: "Why do you look up into the sky so much? Do you learn anything?"

Jesus thought for a while before he answered: "The stars are like windows through which light comes to give us hope. They can teach us much. They can tell us many stories. They can give us insight. To travelers, a star is a light to guide them. To those upon the waters, the stars are sources of strength and encouragement, for they shine with a powerful force. To a mother, a star gives comfort and consolation because when her children have left home she knows they look upon the same stars as she does no matter where they have gone. To an old person, the light from the stars grows dim, but knowing they are still there is a constant reminder that the universe and all within it are guided by my heavenly Father."

Judas asked, "Master, is it not true that your mother received a message from the stars through Amoriatha—a man who had studied the stars?"

Jesus looked at Judas and said: "Yes, he has been a friend to both my mother and me. He has taught me much about the stars."

Andrew said, "But, Master, doesn't the Father tell you everything?"

Peter shook his head at what seemed to him to be a silly question and said, "Isn't it better to have more than one teacher, Master?"

Jesus responded: "There is truth in what you say, for each of us is an instrument to do the Father's work. It is important that we use well the gift of life given to us. If we use what God has given to us for the good of all, we will be great teachers. If we live and teach without feeling or caring, what we do and say will not be effective. Our efforts will not bear fruit."

And then Jesus looked up at the sky once again and said, "The stars are the lights of heaven to guide us, to give us comfort, and to remind us that the Father lives and still watches over us."

A Perfect Night for Stars

It was a cool, clear night—a perfect night to view the stars. Jesus seemed lost in thought as he stared at them. All of his friends had fallen asleep except John, who tossed and turned, but sleep would not overtake him even though he was tired—perhaps too tired. When he noticed Jesus was awake, he said, "Master, is there anything you would like to talk about?"

Jesus smiled because John seemed childlike in the way he asked. Jesus felt like a father to him and answered: "Yes, John. But let's go over there where we will not disturb anyone."

They walked a short distance, and John asked: "Master, what makes a star shine so that it can light the darkness of the night? Did the Father plan it that way? Is starlight a gift or a curse?"

Jesus smiled and answered: "I tell you this, John: The light from the stars gives confidence to weary travelers who cannot find their way. The light from the stars is so bright and yet so dim."

"Master, I don't understand," John said. "How can it be bright and dim at the same time?"

"It is that way with many things in life," Jesus answered. "For example, we know that the Father is here with us now even though we do not see him. He is here and yet not here, even though we see his power, beauty, goodness and love in life all around us—in the waters, in the earth, in the mountains, in stone, in the food we eat, in the animals.

"We hear his voice in the words of others, and we see him in others. Each star is a gift. It tells us that there is hope and love even in the darkest of times or in the loneliest of places. It reminds us that the Father is always watching over us, and it lights the way to his home. The smallest amount of light, like the smallest amount of love, can accomplish at times the greatest amount of good."

The Love of God in a Star

*J*ohn cried out to Jesus: "Master, Master, quick! Look, Master! A star is falling from the heavens."

Jesus smiled, but the other disciples who were wakened from sleep did not. "Go to sleep," one shouted.

"Master, it's a sign, isn't it?"

Jesus smiled and said, "It is a beautiful sight, is it not, John?"

"Yes," John answered. "I've heard about falling stars, but this is the first time I've actually seen one."

Jesus said, "John, the sense of wonder and excitement in your voice is a beautiful gift to me."

Peter complained: "But I'm tired and want to sleep; it's no gift to me. What's so special about a falling star that you have to wake everyone up?"

Jesus looked at Peter and said, "My friend, my friend, have you never experienced the love of my Father?"

Peter got up and said: "Master, that's a foolish question. If I hadn't, I wouldn't be following you now."

Jesus said: "I tell you this, Peter: When I was in the desert, I spent much time in prayer asking why I was here and what my mission was to be. For three days and nights I cried out, but there was no answer. And then the most beautiful feeling came over me. It is very difficult to describe the joy and love I felt. It was more beautiful than the love a mother feels when she sees her child for the first time, more beautiful than the comfort a man feels when he is dying but knows the pain will end soon and he will be comforted in the Father's arms. I realized not only that I was loved, but that I was to give something very special to all humankind.

"This star that has held John in rapture is a gift, for in the falling star he has seen the love of my Father. The mother sees it in her child, the farmer in his wheat as it ripens. Peter, Peter, to experience the love of my Father is a joy no one can describe."

Peter grumbled and sat back down.

Jesus said: "The love of my Father remains forever for some once they have experienced it. It is never forgotten; its beauty dwells within them forever. But for others, it lasts only a short time, like a falling star."

The Creation of Nature

The fire seemed to dance in the night as Jesus watched it. He enjoyed the crackling sound of the logs burning. It didn't provide much heat, but it did help to take away the chill of the night. He also watched the men huddled closely, speaking softly to one another. They had opened their hearts and minds to him, and he enjoyed their company.

The three travelers had come quite a long distance to see him. They asked if they could spend the night with him because there was strength in numbers. Jesus had welcomed them, "Come, stretch out your hands and feel the warmth."

One had said to him: "Master, you know so much about life. I have heard you speak, and so I would like to ask you why the Father created the sun, the moon, the stars, the clouds, and the sky?"

Jesus smiled and answered: "The sun was created to give warmth and love to the earth and everything upon it. It makes everything glow. The moon was given to us so that we would have time to rest, quiet time to remember the love of the Father. The stars are lights to guide travelers when they have no candle or oil. The gifts in this world are many. They did not come about by chance. The Father used the divine rule and created them with love."

The Power of the Mind

A young man who had been following Jesus asked him: "Master, why do you stare at the sky? Each time you look at it it's as though you're seeing if for the first time. You are certainly familiar with it. You also look at the lowliest of creatures as though they were special. I've watched while you've broken a small piece of bread, and you made it seem like you were participating in a great feast. Master, I must ask you, why do you act this way?"

Jesus smiled and said: "My son, if you wish to know, I shall tell you. One of our greatest gifts is the ability our mind gives to us. When I look at the earth, I see life—old and new. Every time I look at a grain of sand, a seed, a rock, or a leaf, I see the Father. When I look into the heavens at the sky, the clouds, the stars, the sun, or the moon, or when I feel the rain, I know that there are still many mysteries.

"Upon the earth there is so much that I can touch, taste, hear, smell, and see. But when I look up into the sky, I must use my imagination. I am filled with awe as I try to reach out and touch a star, or when I am warmed by the sun and wonder how far that warmth has traveled and where it goes during the coolness of night. We can reach as far as our hands will stretch, but we'll never touch a star. There is so much in life that we can see only with our imagination, so much that we touch not with our hand but only with our mind.

"I tell you this, my son: We may one day touch the moon and the clouds. Our knowledge may grow so much that we will be able to open the door to the heavens and all that lies beyond, but we shall not see my Father until our soul rises in death."

We Do Not Live by Bread Alone

J esus sat by the edge of the water as the waves slowly lapped upon the shore. It was a peaceful and pleasant day, a day of rest. Jesus was glad to be able to relax, because he was very tired. All his traveling had taken its toll. Now it was time for him to be still.

John and Peter slowly approached Jesus. "Come," they said, "we have bread. Let us eat. A woman at the well was kind enough to lend us her jar so that we could draw some cool water. Another woman by the name of Anne gave us freshly baked bread, Master. She remembers you and was pleased when she recognized us."

Jesus smiled, nodded, and said, "We don't live by bread alone, Peter."

"I know," Peter replied, "but I am hungry."

John laughed and so did Peter; a smile formed on Jesus' face. Then Jesus said: "When I see the waters, the waves, a sunset, a sunrise, a star, a shaft of wheat, a child, a woman who is going to bear a child, a young man, an old man, I am touched. I feel God's presence, the Father's presence in all of this."

Peter shook his head and said, "When I look at myself in the waters, I see a tired old man. I do not see beauty as you do, Master."

Jesus asked, "Peter, Peter, when you saw your firstborn, what did you feel?"

"I was proud," he answered.

Jesus nodded and said, "When you tasted your first bite of bread, what did you feel?"

"It was good, and I was hungry, I guess. It's been too many years ago to remember," Peter answered.

"And when you see the fruit forming on a tree, what do you feel?"

"I wait in anticipation."

"And when you were fishing upon the waters and your net was full, what did you feel?"

"I felt thankful," Peter replied.

Jesus smiled and said, "Each person sees the beauty the heavenly Father has created in a different and special way."

Then Jesus smiled gently, slowly walked once again to the edge of the water, let the waves wash his feet clean from the sand, and said, "The Father has provided us with so much in so many ways. We should be grateful and express our thanks. Without his love there would be no life, and there would be no salvation. And yes, he has given us the ability to bring life into the world."

Truths from Nature

The Man Who Turned People Away from God

A man stood off to the side, away from the crowd. He listened intently, occasionally nodding his head, but never saying anything. When the crowd had dispersed, Jesus motioned to him. Peter and John were surprised, because Jesus did not usually ask people to come to him. Most of the time they came on their own.

As the man slowly approached, Jesus said: "Welcome. I was pleased that you stayed and listened."

"Do you know me?" the man asked.

A faint smile appeared on Jesus' face and he said, "I know everyone."

The man looked at him in disbelief but did not say anything at first. Eventually, however, he said: "The man you claim is your Father has not given you any riches or power. What has he given you?"

Jesus looked down at the earth, then up at the sky, and finally toward a field of wheat. "He gives to me what he gives to all. He gives me the earth to walk on, the sea to fish, and fields of wheat to eat. He gives me the sky, the stars, the sun, the moon."

The man laughed and said: "We do not see him, we do not hear him, and yet you still claim he exists. If he does, why does he not demand respect, for his power must be great?"

Jesus answered: "His power is so great and his love so bountiful that he does not have to show himself for he is within all of us. You have tried to deny him in your thoughts and deeds. And you have succeeded in turning many people away from him. But I tell you this: You know him in your heart even though your mind refuses to listen to his voice as he speaks to you directly or through others."

The man shook his head and said, "I do not understand."

Jesus responded: "I repeat. Your heart knows and sees the truth."

The man began to laugh again, and Jesus said: "In time, my friend, in time you will understand. The earth will be divided. We may chain one another, but we can never chain the heart or soul."

Then Jesus firmly planted his feet in the soil and said: "There are those who will deny my Father's existence for a long time. But once more I tell you: You can prevent the love of the Father and his gifts from entering you, but you can never eliminate them. For no one can destroy the sun, the moon, or the stars." The man sneered and turned away, but in his heart he knew Jesus was very wise.

Jesus Calms the Fear of a Child

A mother and father sat huddled with Jesus and his friends. Their children were trying to stay awake to listen to what was being said. Jesus smiled gently and held the youngest child close to him. Her dark eyes looked up at Jesus and she said: "I'm afraid. I'm frightened, Master."

"Of what?" Jesus asked.

"Hush, child," her mother said, "hush."

"I'm afraid," she repeated.

"You must tell me what frightens you," Jesus said again. "Do you not feel the strength in my arms? Do you not know that you are loved by many—your brothers and sisters who are here, your mother and father, your uncle, and my friends who are also your friends? Do you not feel our love for you and our protection?"

"I'm still afraid," she answered. Her mother reprimanded her once again and said, "Hush, child, hush."

Jesus pulled the child closer to him and said, "Again I ask, what frightens you?"

She answered: "The darkness. I am afraid someone will take me away."

Jesus said, "Look, my child, what do you see?"

"Darkness," she said. "Can you see? I can hardly see you. If it wasn't for the fire—and it's not very bright—I wouldn't be able to see you at all."

Jesus said: "Look up, child, look up at the sky. What do you see?"

"A star," she replied.

Jesus said: "Yes, a star. When you see a star, you see an opening in the heavens. That is where the Father peers out and the angels have opened a door to look down at you and give you comfort."

She looked at Jesus long and hard and then said, "I don't see anyone."

Jesus replied: "Do you have to see someone to know you are loved? The Father loves all of his children and has given much to us. He has given us water to drink, the fields in which to grow wheat, the sun to give warmth to the earth, and rain to nourish it. He has given us the moon so that we may have peace in the night and reflect on the love of the Father in quiet times.

"His gifts are for both adults and children. He has given us the stars, the beautiful, beautiful lights of the heavens. I tell you this, child: Never be frightened of the darkness, because when you look up, you will see light from the heavens. We are not abandoned, and we never will be, for God's love is always with us."

A Child Sings Like an Angel

Jesus sat under an olive tree, enjoying the laughter and noise coming from some children playing nearby. One boy was trying to sing like his father, who was a cantor in the temple. He faked some of the words, but his voice was beautiful in the simple, sweet, childlike tones that came forth.

Peter said to Jesus: "Master, is it not wrong for him to mock his father in this manner?"

"Peter," Jesus said, "he is not mocking his father. He wants to be like him, and this is the only way he can do it now. To listen to the voices of the young or the old is a pleasant and enjoyable gift, especially when they sing my Father's praises on earth like the angels sing them in the heavens."

"How can this be?" Peter asked.

Jesus smiled and answered, "Have you ever listened to the winds blowing through the trees, Peter?"

"Yes, Master."

"This is their song of love," Jesus explained. "And have you not heard the animals cry out to one another in song?"

"But Master," Peter said, "they are only calling out for their mate or because they are hungry."

Jesus looked at Peter and said: "Often we fail to understand that even a child's crying can be a song to my Father's ears. When a child enters the world, takes his first breath, and begins to cry, it is both a beginning and a beginning of the end. Just as songs of peace are sung to my Father in the temple, so too a mother should sing songs of praise to God while she holds her child to her breast. Everything in life has a way of giving praise to the Father—the winds, the trees, and even the rocks."

When Jesus finished speaking, his followers looked at him with surprise and asked, "Why didn't Jacob allow them to join in his song to God?"

Jesus bent down, picked up a bug from under a rock, and said: "Many times we are like this bug, which crawls under the stones. We hide our true feelings. We give praise with our voice, but it does not come from the heart. It is false and empty praise. Music helps to open us—and he pointed to his head, his eyes, his hands, and his heart, indicating his whole being—but first there must be love within if we are to give praise to God."

Blind to Our Blessings

*I*t was a hot and tiring day. Jesus was pleased that only a few people had come to see him, because there were only a few loaves of bread to share among them. Peter was even more concerned.

An old man asked: "Master, I have been very patient, but I must ask you, where is the Father when you need him? I need him, Master. I need him to speak to me." Jesus was silent as the man continued: "I have many problems. I do not see clearly; part of my field has been burned; the workers in the field are careless with the grain. And yes, this, my youngest son, does not want to be my eyes and my ears or to be a farmer. My wife complains constantly and is not well. This is what I have been given. Where is God when I need him? Why doesn't he listen to me? Why doesn't he hear us? Why does he ignore us? If we are all his children, then I ask, where is he when we need his guidance? I go to the temple, and I read the scriptures. Many there comfort me. But I want to speak to the Father, and the Father alone. If I am his child, then why doesn't he comfort me?"

Jesus shook his head and replied: "My friend, you have many to comfort you. Are you hungry?"

"No."

"Are you thirsty?"

"No."

"Is your wife kind to you?"

"Oh, yes. She complains, but she is a good woman. She has borne many children."

"Yes," Jesus said, "you have many sons and grandchildren. And look, your youngest son has accompanied you. Is this not so?"

"Yes," the old man answered, "but his eyes follow others. He doesn't want to be a farmer, to work in the fields. He wants to be a merchant."

Jesus asked: "Is that so wrong? Did you not follow your heart when you were young? Is this not so?"

The man grumbled and replied, "But I worked in the fields and did as my father told me and as his father did before him."

Jesus said, "Yes, and yet you question where the Father is when you need him. When you prayed for rain, the rain came; when you wanted a son, you had many; when you wanted a good wife, you found one; when you were thirsty, there was water to drink; when you were hungry, there was bread to eat. That is also where the Father's love is to be found."

"Oh," another man said, "my wife was taken. Does that mean the Father does not love me?"

Jesus shook his head and answered: "My son, I speak to you now. Everyone experiences pain in body, mind, and heart. We are children of the Father, and children must learn, not only from love, but also from pain and sorrow. We must also learn that the Father has given us much."

Jesus continued: "Look at the waters. Look at the sky. In the day there is the sun to make the crops grow, and there is water to quench the earth's thirst. There are rocks to build homes, soil to grow wheat, trees to bear fruit. We have the night to cool the earth; we have stars to light the weary traveler's way. This is where the Father is. He is here when we need him; he is with us always. He has created us and given us life and breath. He has given us a mind and talents. God, the Father of us all, the Creator, has given us love. He has given us hope, and yes, through me, he has given humanity a dream, a dream of eternal peace."

Then he looked down, picked up a loaf of bread, broke it, and said, "Share your love with me, and I will share with you the knowledge that has been given to me."

A Storm at Sea

*J*esus sat straight and tall in the boat. The water had a calming effect on him, and the warmth of the sun felt good on his tired body. Peter especially felt relaxed and happy because he was at home in a boat upon the waters. His heart was filled with contentment. Jesus smiled at his friend and said, "Peter, you are truly happy, are you not?"

Peter answered, "Yes, Master. I wish I could always be as happy as I am right now."

And then all of a sudden, a terrible storm rolled in. The sky was filled with large, dark clouds. Waves began to crash against their small boat. Peter was quickly gripped by fear, but Jesus remained calm and said, "Do not be afraid."

Heavy rains and strong winds twisted, tossed, and turned the boat in every direction. And then the storm stopped just as quickly as it had begun. The clouds parted, the sun burst through, and the water became calm.

Both Jesus and Peter were drenched. They slowly bailed the water out of the boat. When the sun had dried their wet clothes, Jesus said to Peter: "We are like the weather, even like the storm that came upon us so suddenly. One moment we are happy and contented, but the next moment we are faced with pain, suffering, and fear, which we think will never end. But it stops too."

Peter said, "Master, are the people who come to mock you like that?"

Jesus answered: "People are divided in many different ways from one another, but they are all one with the Father. We all go our own way through life, but at the end we will all stand together in my Father's home."

The Existence of God

A young man spoke to Jesus in a strong and firm voice: "Master, I have been with you for three days and nights. I have walked with you and eaten with you. I have heard you speak about the love of the Father. But I must ask you, how do I know he exists?"

Jesus answered: "Yes, you have been with me for three days. You have heard me teach, and still you have not found answer to your question. I tell you this: Look at this tree. Why does it exist? Does it not bear fruit? And when it is old and can no longer do so, it will be cut into pieces to keep us warm and to bake bread. And yet many shoots come from it in a continuous cycle of life.

"A stone is a stone, you may think, but that stone can help to build a home or a wall or a path. It can contain fire by encircling it and keeping us from harm. We only need to look at a field of flowers or wheat, or at the sun, the moon, or the stars in the sky. Do you really believe this all came into existence on its own?"

The young man replied, "But you are still not answering my question."

Jesus said, "Look closely at your hands, my friend." And Jesus took the young man's hands and placed them in front of his eyes, turning them from the palms to the backs. Then he said, "You have hands to work with, to bring forth life, to comfort." Then Jesus pointed down at the young man's feet and said: "You have these to walk on and work with. The Father has given us many gifts in the way he has designed life."

Jesus continued: "Listen! Hear the bird? The love of God our Creator is everywhere in nature and throughout life." Then he took one of the young man's hands, placed it over his heart, and said: "He has given us a gift, the gift of life, which is a gift beyond all gifts. Life is precious, even more precious than the water that quenches our thirst."

Jesus smiled and concluded: "I tell you this: Speak to the Father, and great rewards will come to you. You will discover his presence and understand his love when you look around you and within you."

Friendship

*J*esus was pleased. You could hear it in his voice and see it in his eyes. He was going home to visit his mother. Peter and John were happy because he was happy. Even his step seemed lighter to them. When they stopped along the way and sat down to eat, Jesus broke bread, blessed it, gave it to his friends, and said: "Soon we shall taste my mother's bread and visit my father, my aunt, and my friends. I am really looking forward to it. It is nice to be able to remember those you have loved, but it is even nicer—truly a gift—to be able to see them, talk to them, and touch them."

Peter said to John: "I'm glad to see the Master so happy. His family and friends are very important to him."

Jesus overheard Peter and said: "You are right, my friend. The love of family and friends has many of the same qualities as the sun. It is bright and warm and makes life grow."

"But, Master, isn't the night just as comforting?" Peter asked.

"Yes, in many ways," Jesus answered, "but night is a time for resting and for relaxing."

John added: "That's right, Master. It's hard working in the hot sun. When I worked in the vineyards, the sweat seemed to cling to my body until I wiped it off."

Jesus looked at John and said: "My friend, my friend, we remember both the good and the bad in life. We remember our friends. Their friendship remains with us and continues to nurture us even when they have left us, never to return. Friendship is like the beauty in this flower. No one would buy it from you because it grows wild among the rocks. Its beauty is a gift to us from the Father. It is here today and gone tomorrow, replaced by beauty in another form. Its fragrance lasts as long as its beauty."

Tears began to form in Jesus' eyes as he said, "The Father's home sometimes seems like a dream, the earth may be likened to a heavenly song, and in one another we can find the beauty and power of the flowers, the waters, and the stars."

Peter looked at Jesus with many questions in his eyes and said: "Master, you must explain what you're saying. After all, I'm nothing but a fisherman."

Jesus smiled and said: "Think about it, Peter. Think about it."

The Warmth of the Father's Love

*T*was a bright, sunny day, but a cool, gentle breeze flowed from the water below. It was also a good and productive day, for many people had come to listen to Jesus. John said, "Master, I am so pleased with you." The others chuckled.

Jesus replied, "I am pleased that you are pleased, John."

The others laughed aloud, but Jesus said, "I did not mean to be funny."

"Yes," Peter said, "but I am the one brings the crowds to the Master."

The laughter increased.

"Give him time," Jesus said. "Give him time."

John hung his head. Jesus touched his arm and said, "Look up."

And then John said: "Master, the Father is always with you. He tells you what to say, and then he helps you. But what about us? We are nothing but fools."

"But you learn from me," Jesus said.

"Yes," Peter said, "we learn, but how do we know the Father is within us?"

Jesus answered: "Why do you ask that? You should know by now that the Father is always with each and every person."

"With the sinner?" Judas asked.

"Yes," Jesus answered, "even with the sinner. For you are all special souls. Each of you is a gift. You are his creation, his work."

"But some of us fail," John said.

"That is true," Jesus said, "but the Father is always there to help mold you again if you wish to grow in his image through his word."

Then he looked down at the water below and said: "Feel the cool breeze that the water brings to us. Look at the sky and feel the warmth of the sun. That warmth is like the Father's love, and the breeze is like a gentle kiss. Look around you; look up; look down." There was so much emotion in Jesus' voice that shivers ran through those who had followed him. Jesus said, "How can you question whether the Father loves you when you see all around you what he has created?"

There was silence. Not a word was spoken. But there were tears in each man's eyes.

ABOUT THE AUTHORS

CONNIE ANN VALENTI is a mother and a grandmother who sees goodness and beauty in all of life. Sensing God's presence and love in every person and event, she believes that the biblical story of Jesus' life and teaching continues to take on deeper meaning and understanding in the circumstances of our daily life. We are still living the story of Jesus. She has written these stories, told by Fr. Lengwin at the beginning of his weekly radio show, *Amplify*, for more than thirty years.

FR. RON LENGWIN is the founder and host of *Amplify* (since 1975), a two-hour call-in radio talk show on CBS Pittsburgh (KDKA) that touches thirty-seven states and half of Canada and streams live on the Internet throughout the world. The main part of his show is a two-hour interview. His guests over the years include some of the most prominent writers of our time, from Ray Bradbury and Anne Rice to Henri Nouwen and Mother Teresa. Fr. Lengwin also serves as Director of Communications for the Catholic Diocese of Pittsburgh and is a longtime adviser to the U.S. Conference of Catholic Bishops.